THE

FRESH EGGS DAILY
COOKBOOK

THE

FRESH EGGS DAILY

COOKBOOK

Over 100 Fabulous Recipes to Use Eggs in Unexpected Ways

Lisa Steele

HARPER
HORIZON

Unless otherwise noted, photography by Tina Rupp
Pulla Bread photo on page 78 courtesy of the author
Angel Food Cake ingredients photo on page 186 used under license from Africa Studio/stock.adobe.com

Food styling by Cyd McDowell

ISBN 978-0-7852-4543-8 (eBook)
ISBN 978-0-7852-4526-1 (HC)

Library of Congress Control Number: 2021940138

Printed in Korea

22 23 24 25 26 SAM 10 9 8 7 6 5 4 3 2 1

Dedicated to my chickens, past and present.

CONTENTS

INTRODUCTION

Thin tendrils of sunlight slowly move across the field in the still, gray predawn hours, touching briefly on the dewdrops glistening on pink clover blossoms and white daisies. Only the gentle swoosh of a heron's flapping wings can be heard. Then a woodpecker knocks on a pine tree and a chipmunk chides him from a perch hidden high in the branches, as small songbirds trill from their nests, and here and there, bees flit from flower to flower.

I'm still asleep in the cozy home on our small Maine farm, where we've lived for the past seven years, after trading a Wall Street life for rural living.

Suddenly, the relative stillness is punctuated by the shrill "eer-eer-a-roo" of our lone rooster, Sherman. I open my eyes, swing my feet to the floor, grab my jeans and a flannel shirt, and head downstairs. I gaze longingly at the coffee machine as I pass through the kitchen. My first cup will have to wait. Pulling on my boots, I grab a basket and make my way through the wet grass to the chicken coop.

I can hear the chickens softly chattering with each other while Sherman lets out the intermittent, resounding crow. When the flock hears me approaching, the excitement level grows until there's a veritable cacophony inside. I quickly open the small door, letting the chickens out into their yard to quiet them. Then I walk around to the front of the chicken coop and peer inside.

My favorite hen, Miranda, is sitting in one of the nesting boxes and eyes me warily as I approach. She's muttering, as if to herself. She turns her head, maybe asking for some privacy, then rises into a squatting position, gives a small grunt of sorts, and sighs. I hear a dull thud. Reaching my hand underneath her, I feel a warm egg nestled in the straw. I slide my hand out, gently clutching the egg as Miranda hops out of the nest, clucking loudly, announcing to the world that she's laid an egg. She continues to cackle, as some of the other hens join in her celebratory song, and she heads outside to eat breakfast. As for me, I have the freshest egg on the planet for my breakfast.

Heading back to the house with the egg, I can already taste that first sip of hot coffee and mouthful of egg. Now I must decide . . . scrambled, fried, maybe poached over toast? Or perhaps an omelet?

HOW I HATCHED FRESH EGGS DAILY

My earliest recollection of raising chickens was kneeling with my little brother on our back porch when I was maybe five years old, peering over the side of a large cardboard box. Inside were fluffy baby chicks huddling under a lightbulb for warmth. We named them all, of course—I remember Batman and Robin were two of the names we chose, being big fans of the popular television series at that time—and we loved watching them peck at the ground and chase each other or fall asleep all snuggled together.

But about the time the chicks grew up and went outside to live in the henhouse, we lost interest in them. Raising chickens meant more chores, and what kid wants to clean a chicken coop when she could be out riding her bike or swimming at the town pool? After all, chickens were hardly a novelty. Not only did we have a barn and chickens at my childhood home, but my grandparents also had hundreds of chickens on their farm across the street. So I grew up used to chickens running everywhere.

My recollections of raising chickens aren't the most positive. There was the rooster, Bojangles, who would chase my brother and me around the yard every time he got loose. There were the broody hens sitting on their nests, who pecked at our hands so hard when we tried to get the eggs out from under them that we took to wearing oven mitts to do our daily egg collecting. And there was our cat, Mousetrap, who loved to curl up in an empty nesting box and wait for us to bring the chickens their treats of supper leftovers from the night before—he enjoyed scavenging right along with the chickens.

Oddly enough, I never remember selling any eggs to earn extra money as a kid. I did set up a folding table to sell boxes of handpicked raspberries from the patch in our backyard, and I actually earned enough when I was in first grade to buy the neon orange and yellow bathing suit I had my eye on! I guess maybe the raspberries had a higher profit margin and lower "labor" cost. (Even at that tender age, I had some accountant tendencies.)

Fast-forward a few decades to a small horse farm in Virginia, where my husband, Mark, and I lived. It was early 2009, and with the recession in full swing, homesteading and living more economically off the land was coming back into vogue. I decided that I wanted goats. After all, we already had the barn and fenced-in pasture. I could make soap and cheese! And who doesn't love baby goats?

Well, Mark was less enamored with the idea (he had visions of goats clomping on the hood of his truck!), so he counteroffered with chickens. One of the guys he worked with had started raising chickens and was regaling the office with stories about them. I'm not sure if Mark recalled the accounts of my early days and first chicken experiences, but either way, though I wasn't a particular fan, I figured I'd say yes to the chickens and then work on him regarding the goats. Before he could change his mind (or before I could change mine), I grabbed the car

keys and we headed to the feedstore to pick out six peeping balls of fluff. As we drove home with our box of chicks, I marveled at the fact that it was the first time in more than twenty years that I had held a chick in my hands.

After leaving the small town in Massachusetts where I grew up and graduating from college in Rhode Island with a degree in accounting, like many small-town kids, I knew there was a big world out there I wanted to be a part of. And with that, I moved to New York and ended up spending the next couple of years working on Wall Street. What a whirlwind of cocktail hours and client dinners, movie premieres and celeb sightings. My entire closet consisted of business suits, conservative Ann Taylor dresses, and of course the ubiquitous little black dress. I'm fairly certain half of my wardrobe was, in fact, black. I wore heels and pantyhose. I carried a briefcase. I spent my money as soon as I earned it. And after not too long, I realized that as exciting and fast-paced as it all was, it wasn't the life for me. I always felt like an imposter in that world. And it was exhausting. Town cars home after working twelve-plus-hour days, lunches gobbled down at my desk. And a nearly hour-long commute each way on days I didn't use the limo service. It wears on a girl!

One morning, I took the 7:27 train from Rockville Centre, Long Island, into Manhattan. I stopped to buy a cranberry orange muffin and a coffee from my favorite street vendor. Wearing the Wall Street "uniform" of the day—a navy-blue two-piece suit with a cream-colored blouse underneath, my nails manicured and my hair in a sensible, classic pageboy—I trekked the few blocks from Penn Station to my Midtown office at Morgan Stanley. I grabbed a copy of the *New York Times* from the newsstand in the lobby of the building and then headed to the elevator. Once ensconced at my desk, I sat down, spread out the newspaper, and munched on a piece of muffin, following it with a sip of coffee.

As I bent over to unlace my sneakers and change into the high-heeled pumps I kept in my bottom desk drawer, I stopped. This was not me. This was not how I was meant to spend my life. I straightened up and looked around at all the traders in their suspenders and crisp white shirts. Listened to the faint sounds from the nearby trading floor and watched the stock prices on the ticker tape flash by on the overhead screen.

Picking up my phone, I called my boss, who hadn't yet arrived that morning, and left a message on his voice mail that I was quitting. Then I gathered up my muffin and coffee, grabbed my briefcase, and headed back to Penn Station to catch the next train back to Long Island. My Wall Street career was over. Seven years after graduating from college and moving to New York, I was officially leaving the rat race.

I had, fortuitously, saved up my Christmas bonus and tax refund that year, so I had a little bit of a financial cushion. On sort of a whim I decided to open a bookstore next to the train station in Rockville Centre. Specializing in used paperbacks, my bookstore began to do quite a brisk business not long after it opened. I had recognized the potential customer base of commuters who read incessantly during the long train rides, plowing through novel after novel (this was before the days of the internet and cell phones, so surfing to pass the time wasn't an option yet). By selling used books in that particular location, I offered the scads of train riders an option for more affordable and convenient books. A lifelong, avid reader myself, I was in heaven, delighting in my new "career" choice. Surrounded by books all day, chatting with fellow book lovers—what could be better? And my business background served me well. After all, I knew how to calculate profit margins and overhead and do my own taxes.

But you know what they say about best-laid plans? Several years later, I met the man who would soon become my husband. Mark was in the navy, stationed in Pensacola, Florida, but coincidentally we had both grown up in Massachusetts, barely forty-five minutes from each other, and had mutual friends. When we realized it was getting serious and we were going to get married, I knew I would have to move to Florida, since his relocating wasn't an option. So I sold the bookstore. After two years in Florida, his next tour of duty was in Virginia, and that's when chickens reentered my life. Where my time used to be measured by the opening and closing bell of the stock exchange, all of a sudden it was instead measured by the crow of a rooster.

Oddly enough, things with the chickens were different this time around. I was instantly enamored with them. My chickens were so soft and beautiful. They were funny to watch as they scratched in the dirt or chased each other, clucking merrily. Maybe because I spent so much time with them when they were young, they grew to be friendly and affectionate. There was no need for oven mitts to collect eggs. My hens were sweet and seemed to genuinely like me—and I liked them.

Facebook was starting to get popular, so I launched a page to post all my chicken photos (my friends were beginning to tire of my personal page being inundated with them). I randomly pulled the name "Fresh Eggs Daily" out of a hat. I soon realized I'd retained much of what I'd learned about chickens while I was growing up, and a lot of people who were new to chickens were looking for answers to their questions. My advice was different from the advice of others because I had made a vow to raise my chickens naturally, using herbs and edible flowers and natural preventives and remedies—after all, we were eating their eggs! So my Facebook page quickly grew to 10,000 followers, then to 100,000, then to 500,000 with no signs of slowing down.

I set up a blog, also titled *Fresh Eggs Daily*, mainly as an archive of sorts. I found myself answering the same questions repeatedly on Facebook and thought if I wrote up answers to the most common ten or twenty questions, it would be easy to grab the link from my blog to share anytime anyone asked a question. That was in 2012. To date, I have written over six hundred blog posts, my blog has been viewed more than fifty million times, and I still have more ideas swirling around in my head of topics to write about.

In between the blogging and social media (of course I branched out to Instagram, YouTube, Pinterest, and Twitter as well), I went on to write six books on raising backyard flocks, making me one of the most prolific poultry authors of all time.

My grandmother lived to be ninety-nine years old, and I loved going to visit her in her later years to talk about chickens. She raised hers differently than I do—hers were for meat and eggs, they didn't all have names, and she certainly didn't hang curtains in her chicken house! Even so, I know she was delighted that I was carrying on our family tradition. (I am officially the fifth generation of women in my family that we can trace back to keeping chickens!) Sadly, she passed away several years ago, but she left me with loads of sage advice, countless memories, several family recipes, and of course that chicken-keeping DNA!

The years went by, and I launched a natural poultry supplement line, hosted a local TV show, and continued to raise chickens and share my experiences on my blog and social media. But something was missing. I finally realized that I wasn't living my passion. Sure, I loved my chickens, I loved raising them, and I was good at it, but my true passion is—and

always has been—cooking and especially baking. I binge-watch hours of the Food Network, know the difference between wet and dry measures, and own all kinds of fairly odd kitchen implements like a cherry pitter and popover pans. I realized that I had a cookbook inside of me dying to come out.

My mom had me helping her in the kitchen as soon as I could hold a wooden spoon, and I've been cooking eggs for years. Baking cakes, cupcakes, and cookies; whisking and scrambling and poaching. I've perfected my hollandaise sauce and make a scrumptious crème brûlée. My popovers pop and my soufflés rise. And over the years, I've had to come up with some unique and creative ways to use eggs because as any chicken keeper knows, when your hens are laying, you'll have more eggs than you know what to do with.

I decided that I wanted to share all of that with you. My recipes are a blend of my Scandinavian background (both sets of grandparents came from Finland, thus my affinity for cardamom and dill), my New England upbringing, and my current home in Maine. I cook fresh, local, and seasonal as much as possible. And we eat a *lot* of eggs. Naturally.

I believe that in life you make a series of decisions that ultimately lead you exactly where you are meant to be. And I am right where I belong. Living on a farm, raising chickens. Sure, I miss putting on that little black dress and high heels every once in a while. But I'm much more comfortable wearing a flannel shirt, jeans, and muck boots, with my hair in a ponytail.

Oh, and we never did get the goats.

KNOW YOUR EGGS

Of course, not everyone is lucky enough (or wants) to raise their own chickens. And I do recognize the irony in that statement, because it wasn't too many generations ago that nearly everyone did raise their own flock. At least in rural areas. But it was considered a poor man's venture, while the urban wealthy had the "luxury" of purchasing their eggs from the supermarket. Then times changed, and raising chickens declined once supermarkets became more popular and accessible to everyone and egg prices dropped. But raising chickens has become popular again, whether it's to experience the simplicity of rural life, to know where your food comes from, or to enjoy the convenience and luxury of fresh eggs.

ARE FRESH EGGS REALLY BETTER?

But *are* fresh eggs really better? Is it worth getting up at the crack of dawn to brave the elements and pilfer eggs from broody chickens? I can verify firsthand that it's all worth it, and I highly recommend always cooking with and eating the freshest eggs possible. It does make a difference. After your first bite of egg from a happy, healthy backyard chicken who fills up on weeds and grasses, bugs, and edible flowers and herbs, you'll immediately understand the difference. But that doesn't mean you need chickens of your own. I'm going to share with you how to ensure that you're buying the freshest eggs you can. But first, I need to explain exactly why fresh eggs really are better.

Returning to the house, I kick off my boots and finally pour myself a cup of coffee, adding a generous splash of cream. Grabbing a sip of the steamy brew, I quickly rinse the still-warm egg under the faucet, making sure the water is slightly warmer than room temperature to prevent bacteria from being pulled into the egg through the pores in the shell as I wash it. If I weren't going to be eating this egg right away, I wouldn't wash it at all this morning. I would wait until just before using it. Eggs have a natural coating on the shell called the cuticle, or "bloom," that keeps them fresher longer by acting as a barrier against air and bacteria, and washing removes that coating, so it's good practice to wash eggs prior to cooking them.

I also don't generally refrigerate our eggs. As long as they haven't been washed, eggs can stay out at room temperature for several weeks and still be fine to eat, although they will stay fresher about seven times longer if they are chilled. (Eggs should always be stored pointy end down no matter where you keep them to ensure that the yolk stays centered in the white. This is important when making deviled eggs but also to help protect the yolk from any bacteria reaching it, since the slightly alkaline egg white isn't conducive to bacteria growth like the nutrient-rich yolk is). But we go through eggs so fast around here, they rarely last more than a few days in the bowl on the counter. Room-temperature eggs work better for baking, so I always like to keep some out on the counter for that reason. Plus, they're so pretty! I think every kitchen needs a bowl full of blue, green, tan, and white eggs!

Colored eggshells are pretty, but there's nothing more luscious looking than the inside of a freshly laid egg from a backyard chicken. The yolk of the egg is bright orange, signifying that my chickens gorge themselves on a variety of foods rich in the carotenoid xanthophyll, which gives not only the egg yolks but also the chickens' beaks and feet such vivid pigmentation. Some of my flock's favorites that contain xanthophyll include basil, dandelions, marigolds, parsley, spinach, pumpkins, watermelon, and most leafy greens.

The yolk is round and compact and stands up tall due to a clear membrane surrounding it that preserves the integrity of the yolk and acts as another barrier to bacteria. As the egg ages, that membrane deteriorates, so the yolk becomes more prone to breakage and flattening out. The white of a fresh egg is also thick, not watery. It's cloudy and has a yellowish tint because of the riboflavin it contains. An older egg will have runny, clear whites that spread out in the pan.

But what it really comes down to is taste. Store-bought eggs can't rival the taste of a fresh egg laid by chickens who eat a healthy, varied diet packed with nutritious fruits, vegetables, lean meats, and whole grains. (Yes, chickens are omnivores, not vegetarians. They're as likely to gobble up an insect, lizard, or frog as they are cracked corn or sunflower seeds.)

While a single food a chicken eats won't generally taint the taste of her eggs, the overall diet of a hen does contribute to the general taste. As an egg ages, it loses that fresh taste, although it likely won't lose much nutritional value. However, the chicken's diet also contributes to the nutritional value of the eggs it lays. Studies have shown that chickens allowed to range freely, eating grasses and weeds, will lay eggs that contain, on average, a third less cholesterol, one-quarter less saturated fat, two-thirds more vitamin A, two times more omega-3 fatty acids, three times more vitamin E, and seven times more beta-carotene than eggs laid by the typical commercially raised, factory-farmed hen.

IS THIS EGG FRESH?

Unfortunately, there's no way to tell if an egg is fresh merely by looking at it. But there are some insider tricks to help you choose the freshest eggs.

Finding fresh eggs might be as easy as stopping at a neighbor's house where you see a "fresh eggs" sign by the driveway. Or maybe there's a local farm that sells eggs. It's a good bet that eggs procured either of these ways are going to be fresh—likely laid within a couple of days—because of supply and demand, but it doesn't hurt to ask when the eggs were collected.

A farmers market is another place to find locally laid eggs if you're in a more urban area. Even some of the large chain grocery stores now carry locally sourced eggs. Just because a farm is local doesn't necessarily mean the eggs in that carton are fresh, but there are some simple ways for you to pick out the freshest eggs no matter where you're doing your shopping.

CRACKING THE EGG CARTON CODE

At the grocery store where eggs are sold in cartons, it's very easy to figure out how old the eggs are. Printed on one end of each egg carton, you'll find a three-digit number from 001 to 365, which represents the packaging date. (In a leap year, the number range ends with 366.) The number 001, for example, refers to January 1, 365 stands for December 31. Using this code, you can tell when the eggs were put in the carton, so you'll always want to choose the carton with the date closest to the current date.

Since eggs last for weeks or even months (refrigerated eggs can remain good to eat with little reduction in nutritional value for three to four months or longer), there's no telling how long that carton has been on the store shelf unless you know how to check the code.

But what about buying eggs at a farmers market or someplace where they aren't in cartons, or the carton isn't coded? In that case, you need to pick up an egg and shake it. If you can feel the insides sloshing around, the egg is old. As an egg ages, it loses moisture through the pores in the eggshell and air enters the egg, creating an air pocket in the blunt end of the egg. That allows room for the egg to move around inside the shell, indicating an older egg. A very fresh egg hasn't had time to allow any air in or moisture out, so the insides don't have room to move.

Another simple way to determine the freshness of an egg is to "float" it in a clear glass of water. A very fresh egg will lie on its side on the bottom of the glass. As the egg ages and air enters through the pores, the blunt end of the egg will start to rise off the bottom of the glass. The egg is still good to eat but is likely a week or two old. As the egg gets older and more air enters, the egg will sit upright in the glass. As long as the egg is still touching the bottom of the glass, the egg is probably fine to eat, but once the egg starts to float, it's best to toss it. Since bacteria often seep into the egg along with the air, I don't like to take any chances with "floaters." Regardless of how old an egg is, if it smells bad, or the insides look discolored, toss it.

Since it's likely that many of you who picked up this cookbook don't raise your own chickens and instead purchase eggs at the store, I think it's also necessary to talk about egg carton labels. You've likely stood in front of the shelf of cartons, your head swimming with phrases like "cage-free," "pasture-raised," "organic," and "hormone-free." What's critical when reading an egg carton is to be sure you're choosing the best quality eggs laid by the happiest chickens.

Let's start with what you can ignore.

Descriptors like "all-natural" and "farm-fresh" are purely marketing ploys and really don't mean anything. "Hormone-free" and "antibiotic-free" are similarly meaningless because it's actually illegal in the US to give laying hens hormones, and most commercial farms don't give antibiotics to their chickens either.

Then there are some phrases that can be confusing. "Cage-free" sounds lovely, doesn't it? Many of us have seen the photos of rows and rows of chickens confined to tiny cages no bigger than a sheet of copy paper. Well, now picture the cages gone and all those chickens confined to a huge warehouse. That's cage-free. Not exactly a chicken's dream come true. "Certified Humane" also sounds wonderful. It does require that the chickens can roam in that huge warehouse, but it allows their beaks to be cut to a blunt edge so the chickens can't peck at one another. Hmm . . . still not getting a picture of a happy chicken?

Two carton labels relate directly to what the chickens are being fed. "Vegetarian fed" does mean that the chickens aren't fed any meat products, but since chickens are, by nature, omnivores, that's not a very natural diet for them (and by default means those chickens aren't outside eating worms and bugs). The "certified organic" label means the chickens were fed only organic feed, which is free from chemicals, pesticides, herbicides, and other unnatural ingredients. The chickens are allowed time outside free ranging, but that time isn't closely regulated and can vary from farm to farm. If eating an organic diet is a priority for you, then by all means look for organic eggs, but note that organic eggs aren't

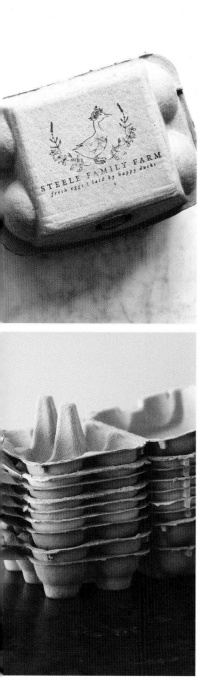

any more nutritious than conventional. Also keep in mind that local, family-owned farms often can't afford the official organic certification, but overall their chickens are eating a varied, natural diet and mostly likely spend the majority of their time outside, so you'll have to decide if that's a trade-off you're willing to make.

Now back to the carton labels. "Free-range" is also misleading. You may envision a field of chickens chasing butterflies and basking in the sun, but in order for a farm to use the term "free-range" on a carton, those warehouse chickens only have to have access to the outdoors. And that doesn't have to be a grassy pasture; it merely needs to be space outside the warehouse or barn. Many chickens purportedly never find the little door to the outdoors, and if they do, the space requirement is sometimes less than two square feet per chicken. Still not a chicken utopia.

Now we're getting to the label you really should be interested in if you want to be sure you're buying eggs from happy chickens: "Certified Humane Pasture-Raised." The conditions for labeling a carton of eggs "certified humane pasture-raised" are straightforward: those chickens must be outdoors on grass or other forage for a minimum of six hours per day, year-round, with at least 108 square feet per bird, and they must have a place to sleep at night that keeps them safe from predators.

The types of pasture that qualify vary widely: some flocks are rotated regularly onto new ground, while others have both fields and wooded areas in which to graze, but their pasture must have some type of vegetation on it. Overall, these chickens are treated the best. If you're at all concerned about the health and welfare of the chicken that laid the eggs you're eating, please look for "Certified Humane Pasture-Raised" on the carton.

WHITE OR BROWN EGGS? DOES IT MATTER?

Growing up, I ate brown eggs. My grandparents ran an honest-to-goodness chicken farm and also owned a diner they supplied with meat and eggs from their flock. For that reason, they raised "dual purpose" or heritage chickens, meaning that while the hens laid eggs, the breed was large enough that a chicken would also make a hearty Sunday dinner. Most of these types of chickens lay brown eggs.

Conversely, most eggs sold in grocery stores up until very recently have been white. The reason for this is that the Leghorn, which is a small Mediterranean breed, has a much lower feed conversion ratio, meaning that less feed is needed for the chicken to produce each egg, which translates to a lower feed bill for the commercial farm.

The perception used to be that poor farmers ate brown eggs, while the wealthy who didn't raise chickens bought the white eggs, and that somehow white eggs were superior. The reality is, the shell color has no bearing on the nutritional value of an egg. Brown eggs and white eggs taste the same and look exactly the same inside when you crack them open—as do green or blue eggs for that matter. Things gradually changed over the years until brown eggs were viewed as fresher and coming from local farms, and they not only began appearing on grocery store shelves, but they were also sold at a premium. Bottom line: Shell color is nothing more than personal preference. I don't care what color the egg is that I'm eating, as long as it's fresh!

COOKING WITH EGGS

If I haven't convinced you yet to raise some chickens in your backyard, I hope I've at least convinced you to seek out the freshest, most nutritious eggs you can. Will eggs from your backyard flock save you money? Absolutely not. As my husband constantly reminds me, these are the most expensive eggs we'll ever eat. When you factor in the cost of the baby chicks, the feed cost, the initial start-up costs of building or buying a coop and erecting a pen or run, plus any supplements or treats that you feed them, you'll never beat the cost of eighteen eggs for eighty-nine cents at one of the shopping clubs, or likely two or three dollars a dozen at the supermarket for "premium" eggs. But fresh eggs are worth every penny.

My stomach growls, reminding me that I haven't eaten yet, so I slip a pat of butter into the skillet on the stove and turn on the flame. Once the butter stops sizzling, I crack the egg on the counter and slide it into the pan.

Within a minute or two, my egg is cooked. The whites are set and slightly crispy around the edges, and the yolk is partially cooked but still runny in the middle. I tilt the skillet, and the egg slides out of the pan onto my plate. It needs no seasoning, but a slight sprinkle of kosher salt on top elevates the egg's natural flavors.

I press the tines of my fork into the yolk, which splits open to release a glorious, thick, orange gush of liquid gold that lazily oozes out onto my plate. I'm going to enjoy my breakfast now, and then I'll share a few tricks with you to help you get the best results possible when you're cooking with fresh eggs.

It's said that the folds in a chef's white hat (or toque) represent the number of ways that chef can prepare eggs—with one hundred being the gold standard to which a chef aspires. I wasn't able to definitively verify this, but I *have* perfected a few of the many wonderful ways of cooking eggs that are handy to have in any home cook's repertoire. And you don't need to be a trained chef to master them.

EGG WEIGHTS AND MEASURES

Most recipes call for "large" eggs. In the commercial egg world, large eggs in their shells generally weigh between 2 and 2.25 ounces. In the backyard chicken world, our girls pop out eggs of all shapes and sizes. Normally this doesn't matter if you're scrambling or frying eggs, but in the world of baking or any recipe that calls for emulsifying eggs, the size of an egg and the white-to-yolk ratio play an important part.

Commercial eggs are graded by size, from small to jumbo. But interestingly, they're sold by weight, not size, and by the dozen, not individually. So, for example, a dozen medium eggs will weigh 21 ounces, or an average of 1.75 ounces per egg; however, the weights of individual eggs in that carton don't all have to be exactly 1.75 ounces. The same goes for the other sizes of eggs: not every egg in a carton of large eggs is necessarily going to be a large-weight egg, and so on.

Egg Size Chart

The chart below shows the average weights of eggs in different size classes, as well as the total weight of a carton of each size of egg. While individual eggs in a carton can vary in weight, so can the average weights of eggs in each size class.

Most of my chickens' eggs seem to fall in the 1.75-ounce range, so technically they're medium, not large, eggs. Thus, your results for the recipes in this book will be closer to mine using medium eggs, but large eggs most likely won't make much of a difference.

Size Class	Average Weight / Egg (in ounces)	Total Carton Weight (in ounces)
Small	1.5	18
Medium	1.75	21
Large	2.0	24
Extra Large	2.25	27
Jumbo	2.50	30

I guess any chicken keepers worth their salt would own an egg scale and weigh and sort eggs before cooking or baking with them, but I can tell you in more than a decade of raising chickens, I've never worried about what size egg I'm using in a recipe. I pick out a few that look to be average-size. But if you want to be precise in your cooking and baking, I absolutely recommend investing in a kitchen scale to weigh your eggs. Most recipes do call for large eggs, so especially with baking, where measurements are more critical, weighing your eggs before using them can help you achieve more consistent results.

If you don't have an egg scale, you can still measure eggs for a recipe. The average large egg contains just over 3 tablespoons of liquid: roughly 2 tablespoons of white and 1 tablespoon of yolk. So if you want to be sure you're using the right amount of egg in a recipe, you can always lightly whisk the number of eggs called for and then measure them out by tablespoons.

A note about duck or goose eggs: If you raise ducks or geese or can procure the eggs at a farmers market or gourmet shop, you can absolutely use them in any of the recipes in this book. I often cook and bake with waterfowl eggs and, in fact, due to their higher fat content, they will make baked goods rise higher and taste richer. Since duck eggs are about 30 percent larger than chicken eggs, you'll have to make some adjustments to the recipes. The rule of thumb is this: 2 duck eggs equal 3 chicken eggs in weight. So if a recipe calls for 3 eggs, you can substitute 2 duck eggs. And with larger goose eggs, 1 goose egg equals 3 chicken eggs. Or to be accurate, weigh the eggs on your kitchen scale or crack the eggs and measure out 3 tablespoons for each egg the recipe calls for. From my experience, I've used some of my smaller duck eggs one for one in recipes calling for chicken eggs and never had a problem. Unless you call lighter, fluffier baked goods a problem.

HOW TO CRACK AND SEPARATE EGGS

Cracking eggs and separating eggs are two skills necessary before we get cooking. Eggs should always be cracked on a flat surface. This prevents eggshell shards from being pushed into the egg, which can happen if you crack the egg on a sharp edge. If you crack an egg on the rim of a bowl or skillet, there's a chance that shell fragments—or worse, bacteria—could be mixed into the egg white and end up in your dish. Holding the egg horizontal, sharply rap it against the counter, roughly in the middle. Then, using your thumbs, pull the two halves apart and let the contents drop into a dish.

If you don't feel confident in your egg-cracking skills, it's always a good idea to slide the cracked eggs into a small bowl first, not directly into your batter or pan, in case a piece of shell falls in or the egg has gone bad. That way you don't ruin your entire recipe and have to start over. It's far easier to fish small eggshell pieces out of a small dish than from an entire bowl of cake batter.

And unless you're super-confident, never, ever crack an egg and drop the contents right into your stand mixer while the motor is running. If the whisk catches the edge of the shell, I can assure you from personal experience, you'll *never* be able to pick all the pieces out of your batter.

Cracking an egg with one hand is more of a party trick than anything else. I don't think I've ever actually had the need to do it, although of course I've tried and can do it in a pinch. But your chances of making a mess and ending up with shell in your bowl are too high to really warrant it.

Separating an egg is also a necessary skill to master. It starts the same way as cracking an egg, but instead of holding the egg horizontal and letting the contents drop into a bowl, you'll want to turn the cracked egg upright and then carefully pour the yolk from one half of the shell to the other, letting the whites fall into the bowl. Another method involves carefully pouring the cracked egg into a funnel where the yolk will get stuck and the whites will drip out into the bowl. And, of course, there's a party trick for egg separating as well. After cracking your egg and gently sliding it into the bowl, you take a plastic water bottle, squeeze the bottle, then rest the mouth of the bottle against the yolk and release your grip on the bottle. The yolk will get sucked up into the bottle, leaving the white in the bowl.

One more little party trick before we move on. Bet your friends that you can tell if an egg is raw or hard-cooked without cracking it open. (Hint: Spin the egg on the counter. A raw egg will wobble as it spins, while a cooked egg will spin smoothly—and longer—than its raw counterpart.)

EGG TEMPERATURE

When baking, use room-temperature eggs and butter when a recipe calls for them, and use cold cream to whisk into whipped cream. Ingredient temperatures matter. Chilled eggs can cause butter or other fats to harden, creating lumps, but you won't have that problem with room-temperature eggs. And room-temperature egg whites whip higher than cold ones. To warm your eggs, let them sit on the counter for about 30 minutes or in a bowl of tepid water for 10 minutes.

However, cooking with cold eggs straight from the fridge is usually fine, and cold eggs are easier to separate.

TIPS FOR BEATING EGG WHITES

Beating egg whites is a basic baking skill that's important to master for any number of recipes, such as meringues, soufflés, and angel food cake. It's not difficult, but it does require some finesse. Make sure that all your equipment is sparkling clean and grease-free. Even a speck of fat can prevent your whites (or heavy whipping cream) from whipping up correctly.

The Bowl

A glass or metal bowl is best for beating egg whites. Plastic bowls can have a residual film of grease on them. And remember that your egg whites will increase six to eight times in volume as they whip, so be sure your bowl is big enough.

The Utensils

To ensure that your bowl, whisk, paddle, spatula, and other tools you're using are free of any fats or grease, simply wipe them down with a paper towel dampened with white vinegar or half a lemon, or swish them in a dishpan full of white vinegar, then wipe them clean or rinse with warm water and let them dry.

The Sugar

A meringue recipe often will call for superfine sugar because the smaller granules incorporate better into the whites, resulting in a smoother consistency. But if you don't have superfine sugar, you can use an equal amount of granulated sugar, whirled briefly in a coffee grinder or food processor to pulverize it.

The Egg Whites

As I mentioned earlier, cold eggs separate more easily than warm eggs, so separate each egg right from the refrigerator. However, room-temperature eggs whip up better than cold ones, so once you've separated your egg whites, let them sit out on the counter for about 30 minutes.

Separate the egg whites into a small cup or bowl. This will prevent accidents, such as tiny bits of yolk or eggshell mixing in with the whites. It's far easier to pick a piece of shell out of a small bowl than a larger one. Don't use your hands to separate the egg; instead, use the eggshell half to prevent any oils on your hands from getting into the whites. Once you've separated the egg whites, pour them from the small bowl into your mixing bowl. Then separate the next egg the same way.

When you're ready to beat your egg whites, use an electric mixer with a whisk attachment or whisk beaters. Whip on medium for 30 to 45 seconds until the whites become foamy, then increase the speed to medium-high and whisk for 2 to 3 minutes more for soft peaks. At the soft peak stage, the eggs are no longer frothy; instead, they're thick and white, but when you pull the whisk out of the whites, the peaks won't hold up. They will flop over or droop and sink back into the bowl. Keep whipping for about 3 minutes, until you have firm peaks that still curl over when you remove the whisk. Beat for 2 more minutes (5 to 6 minutes total) for stiff peaks. At the stiff peak stage, the peaks will hold when you lift the whisk out of the bowl and on the whisk itself. The whites should be glossy, not dry looking. Overwhipped egg whites will become gritty, dry out, and eventually separate.

If you're adding sugar to your egg whites, this should be done once your whites get to the soft peak stage, starting only when your egg whites have almost doubled in volume. Pour the sugar in slowly so you don't deflate the whites. For the most volume and smoothest texture, make sure the sugar has been fully incorporated and the mixture is no longer gritty before adding more sugar. You can tell by rubbing some of the mixture between your fingers. Incorporating the sugar could take 6 to 8 minutes from start to finish.

Adding cream of tartar, lemon juice, vinegar, or salt to your egg whites will result in more stable whites, but regardless, beaten egg whites should be used immediately so they retain their structure.

GENERAL COOKING TIPS

Whether you're cooking with your own eggs or not, a chicken somewhere worked very hard to lay those eggs, so out of respect for the chicken, if nothing else, pair them with the freshest, ingredients possible. The flavor of eggs is so subtle that it complements a wide variety of flavors, but that also means that a light hand should be used when seasoning or pairing eggs with other stronger-tasting ingredients, to let the egg flavor peek through. So, no cutting corners when you're cooking from this book, promise? If a recipe calls for freshly squeezed lemon juice, squeeze that lemon!

Here's a tip for citrus: I buy both lemons and limes by the bag when they're on sale and slice some, halve some, quarter some, and leave some whole. Then I pop them all into the freezer. The frozen slices and quarters are ideal to chill beverages on a hot summer day or thawed to garnish cocktails or squeeze over fish or a salad; the halves quickly defrost and can be juiced. The whole frozen citrus can be used for grated peel as needed—frozen citrus is much easier to grate than fresh. This way my citrus lasts longer, and I always have as much "fresh" juice and peel on hand as I need.

Everyone should keep good-quality kosher salt on hand and grind peppercorns to order instead of using pre-ground. And why not try green peppercorns instead, or white pepper? Experimenting with different types of pepper can add variety to your meals very easily and inexpensively. I also use freshly ground nutmeg. The flavor and quality of many ingredients, especially spices, deteriorate once they're in powdered or ground form, so buying them whole and grinding as much as you need on demand makes sense. It's also often less expensive to buy whole spices in bulk.

If you're still using vanilla extract, why not try switching that out for vanilla bean paste? Even good-quality vanilla extract can't compete with the lovely paste. Used in a one-for-one substitution in any recipe that calls for vanilla extract, the paste gives cheesecake, crème brûlée, and homemade ice cream those beautiful dark flecks that you would get from using a real vanilla bean (but far less expensively), and there's less of that alcohol taste you sometimes get from extract.

As for dairy items, I use whole milk and cream and unsalted butter, and I always purchase cheese by the block and grate or shred as I need it. Commercially shredded cheese is treated with an anticlumping agent, but that agent can mess up your recipes. Freshly grated cheese will also taste, well, freshly grated.

Herbs should be sourced fresh as well, if possible. It's not hard to grow herbs, nor does it take much space to do so. My tip is to buy the whole plant in the plastic pot, if available. It's not only more economical to buy the plant versus prepackaged herbs, but whatever you don't use can be set on a sunny windowsill, then pruned and trimmed as needed. As long as you occasionally water them, most herbs thrive with little attention. I have a small "patio" kitchen herb garden in the summer months where I grow the culinary herbs I use most: basil, dill, mint, parsley, rosemary, sage, tarragon, and thyme. Then I dry some of the extra herbs to store and use through the winter. Before the first frost, I also bring a couple of plants indoors to keep on my kitchen windowsill during the winter, and I grow some herbs from seed in small pots. It's so useful to have fresh herbs year-round to flavor and garnish

dishes. If you don't want to grow your own, most grocery stores stock a variety of fresh herbs.

And here's another trick. Don't toss the root ends
when you chop scallions. Stick them into a shot glass
full of water on the kitchen counter. They will grow
three or four times, and for weeks you'll have fresh
scallions at your fingertips for the price of one bunch!
Sprinkling chopped scallions on top of a dish immediately gives it a boost of color and a pop of flavor.

I'm a big fan of mise en place. For the uninitiated,
"mise en place" is a French term that means "put in
place" or "everything in its place." In cooking or baking it refers to assembling your ingredients before you
even turn on the stove. It's good practice to gather, measure, and prep (chop, peel, slice, etc.)
all your ingredients before you start cooking, using condiment dishes, measuring cups and
spoons, and so forth. This is important for two reasons. First, you will know you have all
the ingredients you need for the recipe before you get started (or can look for substitutions
for those ingredients you don't have!). There's nothing worse than getting halfway through
a recipe and realizing that you don't have a critical ingredient. Second, when you get to the
end of the recipe, you will know by your empty prep containers that you've added the correct
amount of each ingredient and haven't missed a step! I can't tell you how many times I've
wondered if I've already whisked the salt into the flour—for example, as I'm pouring it into
my cake batter.

Speaking of cake batter, when measuring flour for a recipe you're baking, weighing your
flour is the most accurate way to be sure you're using consistent amounts. But short of that
(I'll admit that while I have a kitchen scale, I almost never use it), spooning the flour into
your measuring cup—instead of scooping out the flour with the cup, which can pack it more
tightly—and then leveling it off with a butter knife or chopstick is going to net you the most
accurate measure.

When I bake, I use my stand mixer 99 percent of the time, so that's what I've used
for the recipes in this book. If you don't have a stand mixer, you can use a hand mixer
in all of the recipes. My mom always used a hand mixer and would give my brother and
me each a beater to lick when she was done mixing cake or cookie batter. I wonder what

mothers do these days. Let the kids fight over the lone paddle of a stand mixer? Or maybe eating raw cookie dough has gone the way of riding a bicycle without a helmet or drinking out of a garden hose.

One final note: Despite the times listed for the recipes in this book, a cook or baker needs to recognize that a dish is done when it's done. Learning what dishes should look, feel, and smell like is a far more valuable skill than being able to set a timer and walk away. A famous chef once said he hated being asked when a dish is done. "It's done when it's done" was his reply. Sage advice that does, however, take practice.

EGG SAFETY

Before we start cooking, I need to address egg safety. You likely have heard that raising chickens or eating raw eggs can lead to salmonella poisoning. Although fairly rare, this is the most common egg-related illness, and some eggs can—and do—contain salmonella, which passes from an infected hen to her eggs. According to the Centers for Disease Control (CDC), approximately one in every twenty thousand eggs could be contaminated with the bacteria.[1] Salmonella poisoning is a very real illness, which in an otherwise healthy individual might manifest as little more than a bad case of food poisoning that causes stomach upset and diarrhea, but it can be serious for the very young, the elderly, pregnant women, or those with compromised immune systems.

Some of the recipes in this book do call for uncooked or partially cooked eggs. Those with compromised immune systems or those who are concerned about food poisoning

---

1. Eric Ebel and Wayne Schlosser, "Estimating the Annual Fraction of Eggs Contaminated with Salmonella Enteritidis in the United States," *International Journal of Food Microbiology* 61, no. 1 (October 2000): 51–62, https://doi.org/10.1016/S0168–1605(00)00375–5.

should avoid eating raw or partially cooked eggs, such as those in mayonnaise and soft-scrambled or poached eggs. Cooking eggs to 160 to 165 degrees (which means fully cooking both the yolk and the white) kills the bacteria.

If you raise chickens, you can mitigate the risk of contracting salmonella by washing your hands after handling your chickens or their eggs, keeping your nesting boxes clean to prevent manure on the eggs, and disallowing your chickens in your house. Discarding cracked or dirty eggs, refrigerating eggs as soon as they are collected, and rinsing them just prior to cooking them will help reduce or eliminate the risk. (Although it's usually safe to store eggs at room temperature for at least two weeks, salmonella bacteria multiply faster at warmer temperatures, so storing eggs in the refrigerator is safer. Eggs should be stored on an interior fridge shelf, not in the door where they will be more susceptible to temperature variations.)

Keep in mind that fresh eggs are less likely to contain large amounts of salmonella because the bacteria haven't had time to grow. As I mentioned earlier, fresh eggs that haven't been washed can stay out at room temperature for a couple of weeks thanks to the invisible "bloom" on the shell that protects the inside of the egg from air and bacteria. Washing removes that bloom, so commercial eggs do need to be refrigerated, since they have been washed, and fresh eggs need to be refrigerated if you wash them. Otherwise, you can leave them on the counter, but remember that one day at room temperature ages an egg as much as a week in the fridge, so eggs will last seven times longer if they're kept chilled. And as I've said before, always store eggs pointy end down. This keeps the yolk centered in the middle of the whites, which not only protects the yolk from bacteria but also makes for prettier deviled and hard-cooked eggs.

BASIC EGG-COOKING TECHNIQUES

Many of the recipes in this cookbook rely on one of these basic cooking methods as the foundation of the dish, so they're all good to have under your belt. I've learned that cooking eggs is a very personal matter. I can't tell you when your eggs are done to your liking. Only you know that, and it takes trial and error. Although it's almost universally recognized that the white should be set and fully white—no longer opaque and gelatinous—other than that, whether you're frying, poaching, or hard-boiling eggs, it's up to you if you want the yolk runny, fully cooked, or somewhere in between.

How long that takes will depend on how high you have your heat turned up. Because eggs cook so quickly, a matter of a minute can mean the difference between a gloriously runny yolk dripping over your toast or a brick-hard yolk. It will take some practice and a keen eye to figure out your sweet spot.

HARD- AND SOFT-COOKED EGGS

I love hard-cooked eggs. I like to keep a container of them in the fridge for a quick, nutritious snack during the day. But the one downside to fresh eggs is how notoriously hard they are

to peel. As an egg ages, air seeps in through the pores in the shell, creating an air pocket at the blunt—rounded—end of the egg that continues to enlarge as the egg gets older. A sliver of an air cushion also forms between the two membranes inside the shell, pushing the egg white away from the shell, which ultimately makes peeling easier. If enough time hasn't gone by to let the air in, generally a week or two, the egg won't peel well.

To combat this problem, you might have heard that you should let your eggs sit for a few weeks and get old before boiling them; then they'll peel fine. And there is truth to that. Or you might have heard that you should add salt or vinegar to the cooking water or poke a hole in the eggshell with a pin before dropping the egg into the water. That also supposedly works.

But forget all you've read. There's no need to add anything to the water, and cooking old eggs kind of defeats the purpose of having fresh eggs from your chickens or the farmers market! Not only that, but older eggs won't be symmetrically ovate-shaped orbs once they're hard-cooked because the air sac inside the egg gets bigger as the egg gets older, and you'll end up with a pronounced dip at the rounded end of the egg. So you won't have pretty deviled or pickled eggs when you use anything other than fresh eggs.

It turns out that the best way to hard-cook eggs is not to boil them at all! You should steam them.

Steamed Eggs

Even the freshest eggs will peel like a charm when you steam them. They'll also be more evenly cooked and creamier in texture. You'll never end up with that weird greenish-gray ring around the edge of the yolk, which can result from either cooking eggs too long or cooling them too slowly. Furthermore, there's less chance of cracks or breakage because they eggs don't get jostled in the pot like they do when they're boiled in water.

1. Heat several inches of water to boiling in a large pot. Turn down the heat so the water is simmering vigorously. Then set a colander, double boiler, vegetable steamer, or bamboo steamer on top of the pot.

2. Rinse your eggs in warm water, then place them in the steamer, making sure to leave room between them so they'll cook evenly. Cover the eggs and start timing: steam 5 to 7 minutes for soft-cooked eggs or 12 to 14 minutes for hard-cooked eggs.

3. After cooking, use tongs to gently set the eggs in a large bowl of ice water for 1 to 2 minutes, until they're cool enough to peel. Roll each egg on the counter to break the shell and then peel off the shell, beginning at the blunt end.

Steamed eggs will last unpeeled in the refrigerator for a week or for a couple of days once you peel them.

Best for: deviled eggs, egg salad, snacking, and pickling

Grilled Eggs

In the summer when you've got the grill fired up, wash a few eggs and stick them on the top rack while you're cooking your burgers or steaks. Turn each egg once or twice with tongs, and after about 10 minutes, you'll have hard-cooked eggs. They won't peel all that easily if they're fresh (although a dunk in a bowl of ice water should help), but they should have a smoky flavor at least, and they'll make a fun side dish at your next cookout, even if you have to split them in half with a knife and dig the insides out with a spoon to eat them.

Best for: nibbling while you've already got the grill going or egg salad with some smoky flavor

Baked Eggs

Similarly, you can hard-cook eggs in the oven. Pop a dozen raw eggs still in the shell into a muffin tin and bake them at 325 degrees. The eggs will take about 20 to 25 minutes for soft-cooked and a solid 30 minutes for hard-cooked. When the time is up, use tongs to carefully place the eggs in a bowl of ice water. Let them sit for 1 to 2 minutes, until they're cool enough to handle. Peel and refrigerate.

Best for: when you have the oven on anyway, cooking for a crowd, or prepping hard-cooked eggs for a week of lunches or snacking

POACHED EGGS

Perfectly poached eggs consist of a pillowy bed of fluffy whites encasing a golden orange, runny yolk, and the key to a good poached egg is, of course, fresh eggs. The whites of fresh eggs are much thicker and more cohesive than the whites of old eggs, and that's critical when you're poaching an egg. You need the whites to hold together in the water as the egg is cooking. In fact, duck eggs, with their super-thick, gloopy whites, actually poach the best!

While some might claim that adding salt or vinegar to the poaching water will result in perfectly poached eggs, I beg to differ. I have tried both methods. I haven't found that salt makes much of a difference as far as holding the egg white together, and while the addition of a splash of vinegar to the cooking water forced the whites to pucker and form a tighter layer around the yolk, it also seemed to result in a weird texture. However, I couldn't taste the vinegar in the poached egg, which I expected to. But in my opinion, neither salt nor vinegar are necessary. Instead, my method of swirling the water in the pot works like a charm.

How to Poach an Egg with the Swirl Method

1. Fill a deep pot or saucepan with 4 to 5 inches of water and bring to a boil, then turn the heat to low so the water is barely simmering.
2. Carefully break an egg into a small bowl. Next, use a wooden spoon to swirl the water in the pot, making a whirlpool. Then stop swirling and, holding the bowl close to the water level, gently slide the egg into the water in the center of the pot. Resume swirling for 1 minute around the edge of the pot, keeping the egg centered in the water.
3. Cook for 2 additional minutes, then gently remove the egg with a slotted spoon. Carefully flip the egg over onto a plate for the neatest presentation and repeat with the remaining eggs.

Your end result after about 3 minutes will be a poached egg with a silky golden yolk with a runny inside that's barely set around the edges. Season with salt and pepper and serve.

Once you master this technique and the timing, you'll be able to swirl an egg, move it to the outside edge, swirl another, move it, and cook several eggs in quick succession instead of waiting until the first is done to add the next.

Note: if you're cooking for a crowd, add salt or vinegar to the cooking water and see what you think, since individually swirling a large number of eggs can be labor intensive.

Best for: weekend Eggs Benedict (page 54) or a simple dropped egg on toast

Coddled Eggs

Coddled eggs are an easy way to cook for a crowd. They're similar to poached eggs except that the eggs are cooked in individual ramekins in a water bath instead of a big pot of water, resulting in a contained egg that's both creamy and smooth. The richness of the egg is enhanced by the fresh butter and heavy cream in this recipe, which, due to the ease of cooking and the sophisticated presentation, is a wonderful way to prepare eggs for a large group for brunch.

HOW TO CODDLE AN EGG

1. Grease your ramekins with butter and set them in a roasting pan or large, wide pot on the stove, using 2 burners if necessary.
2. Add water to the pan or pot until it comes halfway up the sides of the ramekins. Bring the water to a gentle simmer, making sure the water doesn't splash into the ramekins.
3. Pour 1 tablespoon of heavy cream into each ramekin to cover the bottom, then crack 1 egg into each. Cover the pan or pot and cook until the egg white is set and the yolk is still runny, 6 to 8 minutes.
4. Season with salt and pepper and serve.

Best for: cooking for a crowd, or making an easy eggs Benedict

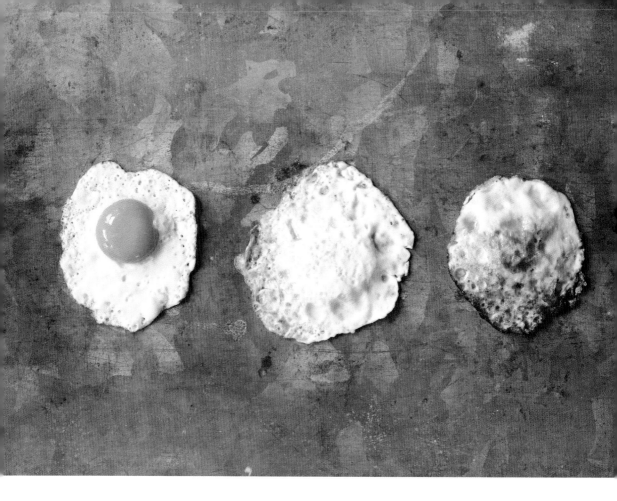

FRIED EGGS

Fried eggs are my husband's favorite. I think he'd be happy eating a fried egg, bacon, and buttered toast three times a day, and that sort of becomes our default dinner when I don't have anything defrosted and we haven't been grocery shopping in a while. So I've had a lot of experience cooking the perfect fried egg over the years.

Fresh eggs are best for frying your eggs because you want the white to stay nestled around the yolk and not spread out in the pan. The yolk of a fresh egg is also less likely to break than the yolk of an older egg, which makes fresh eggs ideal for frying. My husband prefers his fried egg sunny-side up: a partially cooked orange yolk centered in the middle of the cooked egg white. I like mine over easy, with the yolk cooked a bit more. Fortunately, it's simple to fry eggs sunny-side up, over easy, and over hard right in the same skillet. No matter which you prefer, eggs should be fried slowly so they cook evenly.

Sunny-Side Up Eggs

1. Melt 1 teaspoon of butter in a skillet or frying pan over medium heat, tipping the pan once the butter has melted to cover the bottom.
2. Once the butter starts to bubble and foam, carefully crack the egg and then slide it into the skillet. The white should start to set almost immediately.
3. Continue to cook the egg for 40 to 45 seconds, then turn down the heat to medium-low. If you want your yolk more cooked, cover the pan for 20 to 30 seconds, until the white is no longer opaque and the yolk is set but still partially runny.
4. Season with salt and pepper.

Best for: a quick breakfast or as a topping for hash or salad when you want a gloriously runny yolk

IS BUTTER OR OIL BETTER?

I prefer to use butter in the pan when I fry eggs, but you can substitute extra-virgin olive oil or use both olive oil and butter. Oil will result in darker, crispy edges. And a combination of butter and oil gives the eggs a buttery, rich taste in addition to the browned edges.

Over-Easy Eggs

Over-easy eggs are a modification of the sunny-side up method for those who want the yolk more cooked. Start cooking the eggs the same way, turning the heat down after 40 to 45 seconds and continuing to cook. After 60 to 90 seconds of cooking, season the eggs with salt and pepper, gently shake the pan to loosen them, and then use a spatula to flip the eggs to cook the other side. Cook the flip side for another 20 to 30 seconds. Season with salt and pepper.

Best for: a quick breakfast or egg sandwiches if you like a slightly runny yolk

Over-Hard Eggs

Fried over-hard eggs requires cooking the over-easy eggs for 1 minute on the flip side, yolk side down. Over-hard egg yolks are cooked through.

Best for: neater egg sandwiches when you don't want any drippy yolk

Butter-Basted Eggs

Here's an alternative way to mimic an over-easy egg, made by basting the egg with butter instead of flipping it. You'll need to add more fat to the pan initially and cook the egg more slowly over low heat. Start with 1 tablespoon of butter—instead of the teaspoon for the over-easy egg—and heat on medium-low until the butter is melted and foamy, then add your egg. As the egg cooks, tilt the pan, scoop up some of the butter with a spoon, and pour it over the egg. Continue to baste and cook the egg for 2 to 3 minutes for a softish yolk. Baste the entire egg—yolk as well—if you like your yolk more cooked. Slide the egg out of the skillet, season with salt and pepper, and continue to cook the butter for another minute or two until it browns slightly and starts to smell nutty. Be careful not to let it burn. Pour the butter over the egg and serve.

Best for: a decadent breakfast or rich, buttery egg sandwiches

SCRAMBLED EGGS

Now let's talk about scrambled eggs. So simple even a child can quickly master the basic technique, there are as many ways of scrambling eggs as there are people. Some add milk, water, or cream. Some prefer large chunks of egg, while others like their curds small. Some whisk the eggs in a bowl first, and others merely stir the eggs in the pan. Some like their eggs "wet"—less cooked—while others prefer them "dry"—cooked until the eggs are no longer runny. Some people salt the eggs as they're being whisked; others salt them after they're cooked. And many an omelet started with good intentions invariably ends up being scrambled by the time it reaches the plate.

There's no right or wrong way to scramble eggs. It's all about your personal preference, so experiment until you find that sweet spot. Make sure to cook "low and slow" for moist, soft, and creamy scrambled eggs. Add milk or water if you like, but I don't add any liquid to my eggs. According to Martha Stewart, if your eggs are fresh enough you shouldn't need to add anything. And if it's good enough for Martha, it's good enough for me!

TO SALT OR NOT TO SALT, THAT IS THE QUESTION . . .

A bit of science is involved when it comes to eggs. Salt changes the proteins and weakens their bond, so salting your eggs before cooking will make them softer. And salting eggs while they're cooking will cause them to lose moisture, or "weep," and dry out. So if soft or dry eggs isn't your thing, you'll need to wait until *after* your eggs are cooked to salt them.

For fluffy, medium-sized curds and a silky, custardy texture, I swear by the following method of scrambling eggs. Scrambled eggs are perfect for a quick, easy meal, and for teaching kids to cook.

How to Scramble Eggs

1. In a small bowl whisk 2 to 3 eggs until they're frothy. Or crack 2 eggs into a pint-size Mason jar, screw on the lid, and shake the jar vigorously for at least 30 seconds until the eggs are foamy. The addition of air into the eggs results in fluffy eggs, and

it's less messy than whisking them in a bowl with a fork or whisk. The shaking also incorporates the yolk and white much better than whisking does.

2. Melt 1 tablespoon of butter in a skillet or frying pan over medium-low heat until frothy.

3. Pour the eggs into the pan and let them cook until the edges start to set, about 30 seconds. Then gently move them around in the pan with a spatula, pulling the egg from the edges of the pan toward the center. The more you move the liquid around, the smaller the resulting curds will be.

4. Cook the eggs for another 2 to 3 minutes. Remove the pan from the heat while the eggs are still glistening and look wet but aren't runny. They'll continue to cook on the plate, and it's best to remove them from the heat before they're set, so they don't overcook. Season with salt and pepper.

OVEN-COOKED EGGS

Although not as common a preparation as stove-top-cooked eggs, baked eggs are an effective way to prepare large numbers of eggs at the same time. During the holidays, when you're entertaining guests from out of town, or on other occasions when you need to cook eggs for a crowd, why not try baking them? There are several methods you can use for fun and unique serving presentations.

Shirred Eggs

Like coddled eggs, shirred eggs are baked in individual dishes or ramekins, but the egg is whisked before it's poured into the ramekin. Cream, herbs, and meats and cheeses can be added along with seasonings before baking the eggs in a 325-degree oven for 14 to 15 minutes. Shirred eggs are ideal for feeding a large crowd, using up leftovers, or when you need some comfort food.

vitamin C! I've focused mostly on those recipes that let the eggs take center stage. Eggs are nutritious, versatile, and easily accessible, whether they're as close as your backyard or you take a trip to your local farmers market or grocery store. They're plentiful for much of the year to the backyard chicken keeper, although I have been known to hunker down in the coop in the middle of December, pleading with my chickens to lay one more egg, so I can get started on another holiday cookie recipe.

Let's hear it for chickens in every backyard!

PRESERVING EGGS

It might surprise you to learn that when you raise your own chickens, eggs are, in large part, seasonal. It seems to always be feast or famine when it comes to chickens laying eggs. You'll collect more eggs than you know what to do with in spring and summer, but be ready for an almost complete shutdown of production in late fall and winter. That's because the length of the day dictates egg production. A hen needs fourteen to sixteen hours of daylight for her ovary to release a yolk so it can begin its journey down the oviduct. So shorter days result in drastically reduced egg production, and the winter months can be lean eggwise (unless you resort to artificial light, which I'm not a fan of).

While commercial egg farms use artificial light in their chicken barns to force year-round laying, I prefer to go the au naturel route and give my hens a much-needed winter break so they can relax and come back laying with a vengeance in the spring. Thus, I always "put up" some eggs at the end of summer, so I don't have to use store-bought eggs during the winter.

When your hens *are* earning their keep, you'll spend hours surfing Pinterest looking for new ways to use up all those extra eggs; however, when your chickens are on break, you'll curse them as you forlornly reach for that canister of oatmeal from the pantry. For this reason, it's good to know a few methods of preserving excess eggs when they're bountiful to use later during the egg drought!

There are several simple ways to preserve eggs when they are in abundance to store and eat during leaner times.

FREEZING EGGS

During the summer months when egg production is high and your egg basket is overflowing, be sure you set aside some of your extra eggs to use through the winter. I always freeze a few dozen eggs for holiday baking and to use through the cold months when laying naturally slows.

There are various ways to freeze eggs, and all work fine. The one thing you don't want to do is freeze your eggs whole in the shell, because they'll crack and you'll risk bacterial contamination when you defrost them. But you can freeze whisked eggs—whole eggs without the shells, only the whites, or only the yolks.

Frozen whole eggs will last about six months in the freezer. When you are ready to use them, take as many eggs out of the freezer as your recipe calls for and defrost them overnight in the fridge or on the counter. Once defrosted, the eggs should be used immediately and only in recipes that call for them to be fully cooked.

So, here's how you freeze eggs. All you need is an ice cube tray, salt, cooking spray, and fresh eggs.

Freezing Whole Eggs

Coat an ice cube tray with cooking spray (a flexible silicone tray works best for removing the eggs after they are frozen solid), break open and pour each egg into a compartment, then freeze the trays. Once the egg cubes are frozen, you can pop them out and store them in the freezer in freezer bags or a freezer-safe container.

However, the egg yolks' texture might change after the eggs are thawed, so freezing whole whisked eggs is preferred.

Best for: fried eggs, egg sandwiches, or baking

Freezing Whisked Eggs

If you'll be using the eggs for baking or scrambling, you can lightly whisk them with a pinch of salt to preserve their original texture. Coat an ice cube tray with cooking spray, pour the mixture into the trays, then freeze them. Once the egg cubes are frozen, pop them out and store them in freezer bags.

When you are ready to use the eggs, remember that each 3-tablespoon cube of whisked whole egg is the equivalent of 1 egg, so it's very easy to measure out the correct number of cubes for recipes.

Best for: scrambled eggs or recipes calling for whole eggs

Freezing the Whites

If you want to separate your eggs instead, that works too. With this method you can save leftover yolks or whites from other recipes.

To freeze egg whites, drop the white of each egg into a separate compartment of an ice cube tray coated with cooking spray. If you have several whites in the same bowl, measure them out 2 tablespoons at a time. This equals the amount of white in 1 egg. Freeze, store, and defrost as noted earlier. Egg whites should last a year in the freezer.

Best for: egg washes, meringues, or other recipes calling only for egg whites

Freezing the Yolks

To freeze egg yolks, you will need to separate your eggs and very lightly whisk the yolks in a bowl. You don't want to add air to the eggs, so whisk only until the yolks are incorporated. Add a pinch of salt (otherwise the yolks will have a gritty texture).

Measure out 1 tablespoon of the yolk mixture in each compartment of an ice cube tray coated with cooking spray, then place the tray in the freezer. When you defrost the yolks, remember that 1 tablespoon of yolk is equivalent to 1 egg yolk in a recipe. Egg yolks should last for 6 months in the freezer.

Best for: egg washes, hollandaise sauce, lemon curd, pudding, or other recipes calling only for yolks

EGG WASH

I always hold on to extra egg yolks or whites to use as egg washes. Brushed on the top of baked goods in a thin, even layer with a pastry brush prior to cooking, an egg wash helps salt, sugar, or dough cutouts adhere to the top of pastries, and it seals the edges of stuffed pasta or pastry dough. Depending on whether you use the whole egg, just the yolk, or just the white, you can achieve varying levels of shine and color on your crust.

A classic egg wash consists of a whole egg whisked with 1 tablespoon of water, milk, cream, or half-and-half. Using cream will yield the darkest brown crust and the most gloss, while water will result in a paler golden, less shiny crust, and your results using milk or half-and-half will fall somewhere in between. If you have only egg yolks, diluting them with the liquid will result in a darker crust, and using whisked yolks by themselves will yield a dark golden yellow crust. If you're looking for shine but not a lot of color, whisking egg whites and brushing them on top of your pastries will give you some shine without deepening the shade of the crust. Experiment with various types of egg wash to figure out what you prefer. None of them will change the overall taste or texture of the dish.

Egg washes are also used before dredging cutlets or vegetables in flour or bread crumbs when deep frying. You can use whole eggs, yolks, or whites with any type of liquid (or none at all) in this case.

EGG YOLKS

If you have extra egg yolks, you've got what you need to make your own mayonnaise, aioli, and tartar sauce, as well as hollandaise sauce, Caesar dressing, and more yummy, creamy sauces and dressings.

SALT-CURED EGGS

Salt curing is an old-timer's method in which you bury egg yolks in a salt and sugar mixture for a few days, then bake them at a low heat to dry them out. The salt absorbs the liquid in the yolk and inhibits bacteria growth, while the sugar feeds good bacteria. Once they're fully cured, you can grate them and use them as you would grated cheese. Yup, really! Salt-cured yolks can be swapped in for cheese in many recipes.

MAKES ABOUT ¾ CUP GRATED YOLKS

3 cups kosher salt

3 cups sugar

12 egg yolks

Cooking spray

In a large bowl whisk the salt and sugar until combined. Spread half of the mixture into a 9 x 13-inch glass casserole dish, making a base at least $1/2$ inch thick. Press a tablespoon into the mixture, making a depression for each egg yolk you'll be curing, evenly spacing the divots in the dish. Carefully crack an egg, separate the yolk into a small dish, then carefully slide the yolk into one of the divots without breaking it. Repeat with the remaining eggs. Cover the yolks with the remaining salt mixture, then wrap the dish with plastic wrap and refrigerate for 5 days.

On the fifth day, preheat your oven to 175 degrees. Carefully remove each yolk from the salt mixture, brush as much of the crust off as you can with your fingers, and then place the yolks in a bowl of cool water. Gently rub any remaining salt off of each yolk, then pat dry with a paper towel.

Set a wire rack on a baking sheet and coat with cooking spray, then place the yolks on the rack and set in the oven for 2 hours. Turn off the oven and remove the rack. Let the yolks cool, then store them covered in the refrigerator.

Grate the yolks with a cheese grater or Microplane as needed to top pasta, scrambled eggs, soups, baked beans, salads, or anything else you would normally grate cheese over. Salt-cured eggs will last about 4 weeks in the refrigerator.

PICKLED EGGS

Pickled eggs are tasty snacks, but they also make a delicious base for deviled eggs. The flavor of the eggs will intensify over time as they sit in the brining liquid, and pickled eggs will last for three to four months in the refrigerator as long as the liquid continues to cover the eggs. This is my preferred pickling recipe, but you can experiment with other spices if you wish.

MAKES 6 PICKLED EGGS

1 3/4 cups champagne vinegar or white wine vinegar

3/4 cup water

2 tablespoons granulated sugar

1 teaspoon kosher salt

4 garlic cloves

1 shallot, cut into thin rings

1 teaspoon whole peppercorns

1/4 teaspoon mustard seeds

1/4 teaspoon red pepper flakes

2 cinnamon sticks

4 fresh dill sprigs

1 bay leaf

6 hard-cooked eggs (page 23)

Bring the vinegar, water, sugar, and salt to a boil in a small saucepan, then simmer for several minutes to dissolve the sugar and salt. Stir well, then remove the pan from the heat and let the liquid cool to room temperature. You should have slightly more than 2 cups of liquid.

In a small bowl combine the garlic, shallot, peppercorns, mustard seeds, and red pepper flakes. Stir to combine. In a quart Mason jar, add half of the mixture from the bowl, along with the cinnamon sticks, dill, and bay leaf.

Then add 3 of the eggs to the jar, top with the remaining spices and herbs, and add the last 3 eggs. Pour the liquid over the eggs, making sure they are covered (you can add a bit more vinegar to the jar, if necessary), but leaving at least 1/2 inch of headroom in the jar. Screw on the lid and refrigerate the jar. Let the jar of pickled eggs sit for 5 to 7 days before you eat them.

Note: It's not safe to pickle eggs using the water-bath method. They are not shelf-stable and must be kept in the refrigerator.

If the idea of raising some chickens of your own is taking hold in the back of your mind, then you need to know a few things. First and foremost, you don't need a rooster for your hens to lay eggs. Their eggs won't be fertile and will never hatch into a chick, but the hens will lay like clockwork in a rooster-free flock. However, no chicken lays an egg every day. Egg production ebbs and flows with the seasons, and hens only lay well for two to three years after popping out their first egg when they're around five months old. Then their output falls by about 20 percent per year for the next few years, after which they stop altogether. However, a well-cared-for chicken can live eight to ten years or longer, so that should be a consideration as well before diving into the wonderful world of chicken keeping.

Whether you have chickens or not, I hope you enjoy this cookbook. It wasn't until we started raising chickens more than a decade ago that I started searching for other ways to use eggs beyond the typical breakfast dishes. As a result, I've been making my own mayonnaise and ice cream for years, well before we bought our farm in Maine, simply because we had an abundance of fresh eggs from our chickens. So it's become rote for me to make these staples. Since moving back to New England, I have taken advantage of all the fresh local ingredients and included homegrown herbs, locally sourced maple syrup, and Maine blueberries into my recipes.

As a nod to the fairly seasonal aspect of eggs, at least when you raise your own chickens. I've included a recipe index in the back of the book, arranged according to the number of eggs recipes require. So whether you only have one egg or a dozen or only have egg whites or yolks, you can find the perfect recipe. And here's a little secret: have a trusted shortbread recipe as a backup plan for when your chickens utterly fail to come through for you!

Eggs play a role in nearly every baked-good recipe and countless other dishes. In this cookbook I have compiled some of my cherished sweet and savory egg recipes to give you more options for this amazing food that contains every nutrient needed for life except

BREAKFAST

When the sun rises and the rooster crows.

They say breakfast is the most important meal of the day, and I think we all like to start our mornings with something nutritious and filling. A good breakfast sets the tone for the rest of the day. You likely reach for the eggs when you think breakfast, but your choices go well beyond scrambled or fried. I've got more than twenty options for you that elevate the egg to new heights with simple ingredients like cheese, cream, and fresh herbs, but are still quick and easy to incorporate into your morning routine.

Even fairly basic preparations like omelets, poached eggs, and eggs over easy add some variety to your egg recipe lineup. It's handy to learn these methods as well as some foolproof tricks for each. And simple variations on the basics, such as Crispy Lemon-Fried Eggs or Cream-Fried Eggs, will give you more choices each morning as you head for the kitchen.

SWEDISH EGG COFFEE

SCRAMBLED EGGS

Ricotta Scrambled Eggs
Chimichurri Scrambled Eggs
Double Dill Scrambled Eggs
Scrambled-Egg Hand Pies

POACHED EGGS

Eggs Benedict

FRIED EGGS

Fried Eggs with Apricot Jam and Goat Cheese
Crispy Lemon-Fried Eggs
Fried Egg with Asparagus and Hollandaise
Eggs in a Nest
Fried Egg on Buttered Avocado Toast
Cream-Fried Eggs

HARD- AND SOFT-COOKED EGGS

Finnish Egg Butter Spread

OVEN-COOKED EGGS

Cheesy Baked Cream Eggs
Skillet-Baked Bacon and Eggs

OMELETS

Classic French Trifold "Omelette"
Fresh Herb Oil
Asparagus and Parmesan Omelet
Spinach and Goat Cheese Omelet

SWEDISH EGG COFFEE

Swedish Egg Coffee uses a whole egg—shell and all—to brew a better cup of coffee. Somehow the egg white not only pulls the bitterness out of the coffee but also amplifies the caffeine, creating a smooth, velvety cup of java. The egg helps to separate the coffee grounds as well, and the ice cubes act as a French press, causing the grounds to plummet to the bottom of the coffeepot.

MAKES 4 TO 6 SERVINGS

6 cups water

3/4 cup freshly ground coffee

1 whole egg, unshelled and rinsed well

3 ice cubes

Cream and sugar for serving, optional

Bring the water to a rolling boil in a medium saucepan over medium-high heat. Place the ground coffee in a small bowl, and mash the egg—shell and all—into the coffee with a fork. The mixture should look like moist potting soil when you're done.

Add the egg-and-coffee mixture to the boiling water and boil for 3 minutes, then remove the saucepan from the heat. Cover the pan and allow it to rest 5 minutes.

Add the ice cubes to the pan and let the mixture rest another 2 to 3 minutes, until the coffee grounds sink to the bottom.

Pour the liquid through a strainer into coffee mugs, or ladle the liquid off the top of the pan and fill your mugs. Flavor with cream or sugar, if desired. The grounds can be saved and sprinkled in the garden to add nutrients to the soil.

RICOTTA SCRAMBLED EGGS

For the creamiest, most decadent scrambled eggs you've ever tasted, try adding ricotta cheese while the eggs are cooking. This is a way to use up the last bit of ricotta that's been languishing in the fridge. Don't have any ricotta? Try cottage cheese or cream cheese instead.

MAKES 2 SERVINGS

Butter or extra-virgin olive oil

4 eggs

1/2 cup ricotta cheese

Kosher salt

Drizzle olive oil or drop a pat of butter (or both) in a frying pan and heat on medium-low. As the pan is warming up, whisk the eggs in a medium-sized bowl. When the oil is shimmering, pour the eggs into the pan, and move them around with a spatula. Add the ricotta and break it up into small chunks as you continue moving the eggs around. Cook until the eggs are soft set and no longer shiny, 2 to 3 minutes. Season with salt.

CHIMICHURRI SCRAMBLED EGGS

Chimichurri is an Argentinean sauce jam-packed with herby goodness and normally spooned over meat. When it's folded into soft scrambled eggs, it's heaven. The chimichurri sauce recipe calls for parsley and basil, but you can substitute any combination of fresh herbs. Tarragon and dill pair exceedingly well with eggs. I hand-chop the herbs, then finish the sauce with a drizzle of wine vinegar, lime juice, and olive oil. If you're pressed for time or want a smoother blend, whirl the whole thing in a food processor.

MAKES 2 SERVINGS

Butter or extra-virgin olive oil

4 eggs

2 tablespoons chimichurri sauce

Chimichurri Sauce

1 cup fresh parsley

1 cup fresh basil

1/2 red onion, chopped

3 garlic cloves, minced

2 tablespoons fresh lime juice

2 tablespoons champagne
   vinegar

1/2 teaspoon kosher salt

1/4 teaspoon freshly ground
   black pepper

1/4 teaspoon red pepper flakes

1/4 cup extra-virgin olive oil, or
   enough to create a pourable
   sauce

For the Scrambled Eggs

Drizzle olive oil or add a pat of butter (or both) in a frying pan and heat on medium-low. As the pan is warming up, whisk the eggs in a small bowl. When the oil is shimmering, pour in the eggs and move them around in the pan with a spatula. As the eggs cook, continue moving them around in the pan, cooking them until they're soft set and no longer shiny, 2 to 3 minutes. Stir in the chimichurri sauce and divide between 2 plates. Serve with sauce on the side.

For the Chimichurri Sauce

Food Processor Method

In a food processor, pulse the parsley, basil, onion, garlic, lime juice, vinegar, salt, pepper, and red pepper flakes to combine. With the machine running, drizzle in the olive oil and blend until the sauce pales slightly in color and thickens, about 1 minute. Makes about 1 cup.

Hand-Chop Method

Finely chop the parsley, basil, onion, and garlic and add to a small bowl. Stir in the lime juice, vinegar, salt, pepper, and red pepper flakes. Drizzle in the oil, stirring, until you have a pourable sauce.

Refrigerate leftovers and use within a day or two.

DOUBLE DILL SCRAMBLED EGGS

I love fresh dill and grow it in my herb garden each spring. Dill pairs especially well with eggs, and this cheesy scrambled egg recipe also calls for Havarti cheese with dill. My mom and I often enjoy Double Dill Scrambled Eggs for breakfast when I visit her. Not partial to dill? You can use regular Havarti and substitute a different herb. But I'll stick with my dill.

MAKES 2 SERVINGS

Butter or extra-virgin olive oil

4 eggs

1 ounce Havarti cheese with dill,
    cut into 1/2-inch cubes

Kosher salt

Freshly ground black pepper

Fresh dill for garnish

Drizzle olive oil or add a pat of butter (or both) in a frying pan and heat on medium-low. As the pan is warming up, whisk the eggs. When the oil is shimmering, pour the eggs into the pan and move them around with a spatula. Add the cheese and continue to move the eggs around. Cook until the cheese melts and the eggs are soft set and no longer shiny, 2 to 3 minutes. Season with salt and pepper and garnish generously with fresh dill.

SCRAMBLED-EGG HAND PIES

Like to eat your breakfast on the go? Then these compact hand pies are the answer! Any of the scrambled egg recipes in this book would work well in these pies, or you can try the recipe below. This recipe is meatless, but you can easily add some bacon or sausage if you prefer a little extra protein in the morning. The hand pies are versatile, so feel free to substitute the cheese of your choice or add some extra veggies. Leftover pies can be refrigerated or frozen, and then defrosted and reheated briefly in the oven.

MAKES 6 HAND PIES

4 eggs, divided

2 ounces cream cheese, room temperature

1/2 cup shredded Gruyère cheese

2 tablespoons sliced scallions

Kosher salt

Freshly ground black pepper

1 (9-inch) piecrust (homemade or store-bought)

All-purpose flour for dusting

1 tablespoon water

Preheat the oven to 375 degrees. Line a rimmed baking sheet with parchment paper.

Scramble 3 of the eggs in a skillet, following my directions in "How to Scramble Eggs" (page 31). Stir in the cream cheese, Gruyère, and scallions. Season with salt and pepper. Set aside to cool slightly while you roll out the piecrust dough.

On a floured surface, roll out the piecrust dough to roughly 12 inches square. Cut the dough into twelve 3 x 4-inch rectangles using a pastry cutter or sharp knife, rerolling and cutting the trimmings as needed. Arrange 6 of the rectangles on the baking sheet. In a small bowl whisk the remaining egg and the water.

Top each rectangle on the baking sheet with 2 tablespoons of the egg filling, leaving a 1/2-inch border around the edges. Brush along the border with the egg wash, saving the remaining egg wash for brushing the top. Then place or lay the remaining rectangles over the egg filling for each pie, stretching the dough slightly to fit. Press the edges of the rectangles together to enclose the filling and seal, then crimp with a fork.

Chill the pies for 30 minutes. Brush the surface of each pie with the remaining egg wash and prick a few holes in it with a toothpick. Bake until the tops are golden brown, about 20 to 25 minutes. Cool on a wire rack.

EGGS BENEDICT

While eggs Benedict is an indulgent, decadent breakfast, it isn't hard to make. Once you've mastered the hollandaise sauce—the focal point of the dish—the challenging part is the timing: ensuring that your eggs, toast, and sauce are ready at the same time. As they say, practice makes perfect, so perfecting this dish is a wonderful excuse to keep practicing . . . over and over again!

Most eggs Benedict recipes call for ham, bacon, spinach, or other ingredients, but I keep things simple and stick with bread on the bottom (I love a slab of crusty, rustic bread instead of an English muffin), topped with a poached egg and the sauce, to highlight our fresh eggs.

MAKES 2 SERVINGS

4 eggs

Hollandaise Sauce (page 259)

2 split English muffins (or 2 slices bread)

Freshly grated nutmeg for garnish

Fresh tarragon for garnish

Poach or coddle the eggs in simmering water in a deep saucepan until soft set, about 3 minutes. The yolks should be a bit runny, so be careful not to overcook. (See "Poached Eggs" on page 26).

Keep the eggs warm while you make the hollandaise sauce using the blender or Mason jar method (page 259). If using the stove-top method, start the sauce before cooking the eggs.

Toast the muffins or bread slices and place on 2 plates. Using a slotted spoon, place a poached egg on each English muffin half or 2 eggs side by side on each slice of toast, then spoon the hollandaise sauce generously over the top. Finish with the nutmeg and tarragon.

FRIED EGGS
WITH APRICOT JAM AND GOAT CHEESE

My mom knew I was writing a cookbook early on, so she sent me photocopies of old family recipes, her marked-up Finnish cookbook, and any egg recipe she saw that looked interesting, with marginal notes on how to improve the dish. I promised her that I'd include at least one of her contributions, in addition to some time-tested family treasures.

However, she didn't find this recipe in a magazine or cookbook—she created it herself. The goat cheese is a nod to her growing up with her Finnish grandmother, who raised milk goats. The sweetness of the apricot jam serves as a counterpoint to the salty cheese. It doesn't seem like these flavors should work together, but they do. Trust me. Or rather, trust my mother. Mothers always know best!

—————————————— MAKES 2 SERVINGS ——————————————

4 fried eggs
2 tablespoons apricot jam
2 tablespoons crumbled goat
   cheese
Fresh thyme for garnish
Kosher salt for garnish

Fry the eggs using your preferred method. Place 2 eggs on one plate, and 2 eggs on another plate. Top each egg with a dollop of jam in the center of the yolk and sprinkle the goat cheese over the egg white. Garnish with fresh thyme.

CRISPY LEMON–FRIED EGGS

Getting tired of plain fried eggs? Adding lemon slices to the pan while you're frying eggs will add an unexpected burst of citrus that's sure to wake you up! Sunny-side up or over easy, these lemony eggs will be your new go-to for a quick and easy breakfast.

MAKES 2 SERVINGS

4 tablespoons extra-virgin olive oil

1 lemon, cut into thin slices, seeded

4 eggs

Kosher salt

Freshly ground black pepper for garnish

Heat a large cast-iron skillet or frying pan on medium-high. Once the pan is heated, add the oil and the lemon slices.

Give the oil a few seconds to heat up. Once the oil starts to shimmer, carefully crack each egg and slide it out of the shell and into the pan, among the lemon slices. Hold the shell close to the oil to prevent splattering.

Sprinkle the yolks with a pinch of salt and cook, tilting the pan and using a spoon to baste the tops of the eggs with the olive oil.

Cook about 2 minutes, until the whites are puffed and set and the edges are browned and crispy. Remove the pan from the heat (or if you prefer a firmer yolk, flip each egg and cook until the other side is done, about 1 minute).

Slide the eggs onto plates, pour the lemon oil over the tops, and season with salt. Use the lemon slices from the skillet as garnish.

FRIED EGG

WITH ASPARAGUS AND HOLLANDAISE

We used to grow our own asparagus in Virginia, and for anyone who has tried, you know that it takes several years, along with a lot of patience and scrawny spears, before you're finally able to harvest full-size asparagus! We had almost gotten to that point in our garden when we packed up and moved to Maine. I have yet to start an asparagus bed at our new farm, but I do need to, because in the early spring, when the spears are ready to be picked, they're ideal for this dish.

MAKES 2 SERVINGS

Extra-virgin olive oil

6 to 10 asparagus spears, ends trimmed

Kosher salt

Freshly ground black pepper

2 fried eggs

Hollandaise Sauce (page 259)

Freshly grated Parmesan, optional

Heat a drizzle of olive oil in a medium-sized skillet on medium-high. Add the asparagus spears. Season with salt and pepper. Cook 2 to 3 minutes on each side, until the asparagus is lightly seared but still crisp.

While the asparagus is cooking, fry the eggs to taste in a separate skillet. Make the hollandaise sauce using the blender or Mason jar method.

Divide the asparagus spears between 2 plates, top them with the fried eggs, and spoon the hollandaise sauce over it all. Garnish with Parmesan, if desired, and season with salt and pepper.

EGGS IN A NEST

Whether you call it eggs in a hole, eggs in a basket, eggs in a nest, eggs with hats, or simply eggs in bread, this is a quick and easy breakfast option everyone loves. When I was growing up, my mom made this a lot for us kids for breakfast before we headed off to school. I don't remember what we called it, but it was a fun change from dropped eggs on toast, which features a poached egg and no cutout in the bread.

MAKES 2 SERVINGS

2 slices bread

2 tablespoons butter

2 eggs

Kosher salt

Freshly ground black pepper

Chopped chives for garnish

Hot sauce for drizzling, optional

Cut a hole in the center of each slice of bread with a 3-inch biscuit cutter, cookie cutter, or the rim of a medium-sized drinking glass.

In a large skillet over medium-low heat, melt the butter. Place 2 slices of the bread, plus the circle cutouts, in the pan and cook until golden brown on one side, about 2 to 3 minutes. Flip the bread over.

Carefully break 1 egg into each hole of the bread.

Cover the pan and cook until the whites are set, about 1 minute. Continue to cook until the yolk is done to your liking.

Remove from the pan, arrange on plates, and season with salt and pepper. Garnish with chopped chives and drizzle with hot sauce, if desired. Serve with the bread cutouts on the side.

FRIED EGG

ON BUTTERED AVOCADO TOAST

Not all recipes need to be time consuming or difficult to make. Sometimes a few simple flavors combine into something sublime. This recipe is a fancied-up version of the dropped eggs on toast my mom used to make for me when I was a kid. There's something about the combination of eggs and avocados paired with crispy, buttery toast. Don't have any tarragon? You can substitute a different herb.

MAKES 2 SERVINGS

1 tablespoon butter, plus more
    for frying the eggs

2 slices bread

2 fried eggs

1 avocado

Fresh tarragon

Kosher salt

Freshly ground black pepper

Melt the butter in a medium-sized skillet over medium-low heat. Fry the bread on both sides until golden brown, a minute or two on each side. Remove from the skillet and arrange the toast on 2 plates.

Fry the eggs to taste in the same skillet. Add more butter if needed.

Peel and slice the avocado and arrange on the toast. Top with an egg. Garnish with the tarragon, and season with salt and pepper.

CREAM-FRIED EGGS

Forget the butter, oil, or bacon grease next time you're frying eggs for breakfast. These eggs cooked in heavy cream will become your new beloved breakfast. I discovered this method of cooking eggs a couple of years ago, and my world hasn't been the same since! It's a way to use up that last bit of heavy cream and results in eggs that are so creamy, light, and tender, you'll be blown away. Serve over toast or on their own. This is also a good method to keep in mind when you're out of butter.

MAKES 2 SERVINGS

1/2 cup heavy cream
Kosher salt
Freshly ground black pepper
4 eggs

Pour the cream into a large skillet and swirl the pan to cover the bottom. Season with salt and pepper and turn the heat to medium-high. Warm the cream until bubbles start to form around the edges, about 1 minute.

Carefully crack the eggs into a small bowl and then slide into the cream. Continue to cook on medium-high. The cream will bubble, boil, and separate. That's okay—in fact, that's what you want. The liquid will evaporate, and the butter fats in the cream will begin to caramelize as the eggs cook. Turn down the heat, if necessary, to keep the cream from burning.

Cook until the whites are set but the yolks are still creamy and a little runny, about 5 minutes. Remove from the heat and slide the eggs onto plates. Season with salt and pepper.

FRIED EGG ON A BED OF HOLLANDAISE

For an elegant, yet easy variation of eggs Benedict, spoon a pool of Hollandaise Sauce (page 259) on a salad or dessert plate, then gently lay a Cream-Fried Egg (page 66), Crispy Lemon-Fried Egg (page 58), or Sunny-Side Up Egg (page 29) on top. Garnish with chopped chives, scallions, or fresh tarragon, and season with salt and pepper.

FINNISH EGG BUTTER SPREAD

This simple Finnish recipe calls for only two key ingredients: eggs and butter, plus a pinch of salt. Think egg salad with butter instead of mayonnaise. Traditionally served on over Finnish rice pastries, the creamy deliciousness spread on a piece of toast, slathered on warm homemade bread, or eaten right from the bowl with a spoon belies its basic preparation.

MAKES ABOUT 1 CUP

½ cup (1 stick) butter, room
   temperature
3 hard-cooked eggs, cooled
   slightly and peeled (page 23)
Kosher salt

Mash the butter and eggs in a small bowl with a fork until combined but still chunky. The warm egg will help to soften the butter. Season lightly with salt. Serve immediately. Refrigerate any leftovers and use within 3 days.

CHEESY BAKED CREAM EGGS

Similar to Cream-Fried Eggs, these baked eggs are so smooth and creamy, you'll find yourself making them often. They're addictive in their creaminess and also make for a beautiful presentation in the pan. I leave the yolks runny, so I can dip my toast into them.

MAKES 4 SERVINGS

1 tablespoon butter

¼ cup heavy cream

8 eggs

Kosher salt

Freshly ground black pepper

1 tablespoon freshly grated
    Parmesan cheese

1 tablespoon sliced scallion,
    green parts only

Preheat the oven to 375 degrees. Add the butter to a pie dish or an 8- or 9-inch, oven-safe skillet and set it on the middle rack in the oven. Once the butter has melted, swirl the pan to cover the bottom.

Pour the cream into the pan, then crack the eggs and slide them into the pan, being careful not to break the yolks. Season with salt and pepper.

Bake until the egg whites are set and the yolks are partially cooked, about 8 to 10 minutes. Sprinkle Parmesan cheese over the eggs and return the pan to the oven another 2 to 4 minutes, depending on how well you want your eggs cooked. Remove the pan from the oven, arrange the eggs on plates, and garnish with the sliced scallions.

SKILLET-BAKED BACON AND EGGS

More for the presentation than anything, these eye-catching baked eggs truly showcase fresh eggs. If you don't have mini-cast-iron skillets, you can use small ramekins or heat-safe dishes, but the skillets add rustic appeal. And the individual preparation makes this recipe easy to scale for lots of hungry eaters!

MAKES 4 SERVINGS

Brown Sugar Maple Bacon
(page 143)
Extra-virgin olive oil
4 eggs
Fresh thyme sprigs for garnish
Kosher salt
Freshly ground black pepper
Strips of buttered toast for
serving

Make the Brown Sugar Maple Bacon. After removing the bacon from the oven, increase the oven temperature to 400 degrees. While the bacon cools, make the eggs.

Lightly oil the inside of two 6-inch or four 4-inch mini-skillets or ramekins. Carefully crack each egg into a 4-inch skillet (or 2 eggs into each 6-inch skillet). Set the skillets on a rimmed baking sheet and place in the oven. Bake about 8 to 10 minutes, until the eggs are cooked to your liking. (I prefer mine with the yolks runny.)

Garnish with fresh thyme and season with salt and pepper. Serve with Brown Sugar Maple Bacon and toast strips to dip into the yolk.

CLASSIC FRENCH TRIFOLD "OMELETTE"

Omelets are all about technique, and this classic French "omelette" recipe is the perfect way to perfect yours! The absence of filling in this trifold omelet allows the flavor and texture of your fresh eggs to shine. Using only four ingredients—oil, butter, salt, and eggs—you can create a mouthful of flavor by merely swapping out the type of oil. Try avocado or truffle oil to change up things. Cook the eggs slowly and remove the pan from the heat at the right time. The inside should be slightly runny and the outside firm with no brown spots.

MAKES 1 OMELET

2 eggs, room temperature
Pinch of kosher salt
1 teaspoon vegetable oil
1 tablespoon butter

Heat a 9- or 10-inch skillet with sloped sides over medium-high. (It's best to use a nonstick skillet. I love my enamel-coated light cast iron.) Whisk the eggs with a pinch of salt in a small bowl until combined. Add the oil to the pan and tilt it to coat the bottom. Then add the butter and swirl it around the pan.

Once the butter has melted and is foamy, pour the eggs into the pan. Tilt the pan with your other hand to spread the egg evenly, for about 45 to 60 seconds.

When the eggs are almost set, tilt the skillet and, using the tip of the spatula, work around the edge, pulling the eggs away from the pan to loosen them. Then fold one side of the omelet over toward the center, then tilt the pan the other way and fold over the other side. Slide your omelet out of the pan onto a plate.

Season with salt and drizzle with oil or Fresh Herb Oil (page 73).

OMELETS

Omelets can seem fussy, but they aren't hard to make. They're so elegant—and heartier—than other breakfast options when stuffed with vegetables and cheese. For the most tender omelets, make sure to use room-temperature eggs and cook your omelet quickly.

FRESH HERB OIL

This oil adds a fresh, herby goodness to fried eggs, but it's equally delicious drizzled over salads or soup. I like to use it is as a dipping sauce for warm, freshly baked bread. No matter how you use this herb oil, save some herbs from your garden harvest to make a batch or two. Basil, dill, chives, cilantro, mint, parsley, and tarragon all work well.

MAKES ABOUT ½ CUP

Ice cubes
8 cups water
1 tablespoon kosher salt
4 cups fresh herbs
1 cup vegetable oil

Add a tray of ice cubes to a large mixing bowl, then fill it halfway with cold water to create an ice bath.

Pour 8 cups of water into a large pot, season with salt, and bring to a boil. Once the water is boiling, add the herbs and blanch them for 15 seconds. Using tongs, remove the herbs and place in the ice bath for a few minutes until they cool.

Drain the herbs on paper towels or a clean kitchen towel, then roll them up in a dry towel and squeeze out as much water as possible. Transfer the herbs to a blender or food processor and add the oil. Puree about 2 to 3 minutes until smooth.

Line a fine mesh strainer with cheesecloth and set over a large mixing bowl. Pour the herb oil into the strainer and let the oil drain for several hours or overnight. Don't press the oil through the cheesecloth—let it drain naturally. When the oil has drained, season it with salt, if necessary.

The discarded herb solids can be fed to your chickens or whirled in a food processor with oil, Parmesan cheese, and walnuts to make pesto. The oil will keep in the refrigerator for several weeks or can be frozen in ice cube trays for longer storage.

ASPARAGUS AND PARMESAN OMELET

I'm usually too lazy to bother with making an omelet. Even when I start with good intentions, I tend to get impatient and scramble everything together. But when I'm more focused and take the time to make omelets, the combination of the crunchy, raw asparagus paired with the salty cheese is a winner.

MAKES 1 OMELET

2 eggs, room temperature

2 tablespoons milk

Kosher salt

White pepper

1 teaspoon extra-virgin olive oil

1 tablespoon butter

1/4 cup freshly grated Parmesan cheese, plus some for garnish

1/4 cup thinly sliced, raw asparagus spears, plus some for garnish

In a small bowl lightly whisk the eggs, milk, salt, and pepper with a fork until frothy. Heat a 9- or 10-inch skillet with sloped sides on high. Add the oil to the pan and tilt it to coat the bottom. Then add the butter and swirl it around the pan.

Once the butter has melted and stopped sizzling, pour the eggs into the pan. Tilt the pan with your other hand to spread the egg evenly, for about 45 to 60 seconds.

When the egg is mostly set (the bottom should be cooked but not browned), shake the pan to loosen the eggs, then add the Parmesan and asparagus to one half of the omelet, reserving some for garnish. Tilt the skillet and, using the tip of the spatula, pull the omelet away from the opposite edge of the pan. Fold the omelet in half, then slide it onto a plate. Garnish the omelet and serve immediately.

HALF-FOLD OMELET

A half-fold omelet is made the same way as a trifold omelet, but instead of two folds, you'll only make one, right down the middle. If you're going to stuff your omelet with cheese, veggies, or meat, a half-fold omelet will hold more filling.

SPINACH AND GOAT CHEESE OMELET

This half-fold omelet is bursting with flavor. It may seem like a lot of spinach, but the heat from the omelet will wilt it down quickly.

MAKES 1 OMELET

2 eggs, room temperature

Kosher salt

Freshly ground black pepper

1 teaspoon extra-virgin olive oil

1 tablespoon butter

2 cups fresh spinach

1/2 cup crumbled goat cheese, plus more for garnish

In a small bowl lightly whisk the eggs, salt, and pepper with a fork. Heat a 9- or 10-inch skillet with sloped sides on high. Add the oil to the pan and tilt it to coat the bottom. Then add the butter and swirl it around the pan.

Once the butter has melted and stopped sizzling, pour the eggs into the pan. Tilt the pan with your other hand to spread the egg evenly, for about 45 to 60 seconds.

When the egg is mostly set (the bottom should be cooked but not browned), shake the pan to loosen the eggs, then add the spinach and cheese to one half of the omelet. Tilt the skillet and, using the tip of the spatula, pull the omelet away from the opposite edge of the pan. Fold the omelet in half, then slide it onto a plate. Sprinkle goat cheese on top, drizzle with olive oil if desired, and serve immediately.

BRUNCH TO LUNCH

After morning chores, while the
chickens are laying their eggs

Who doesn't love brunch? The word conjures up visions of a beautifully set table piled high with pancakes drowning in butter and syrup; warm breads and muffins bursting with berries, fresh fruit, and sandwiches; and, of course, eggs. These are recipes I generally reserve for lazy mornings when I have more time to spend in the kitchen and linger at the table with friends and family. Time to whip up soufflés or a classic quiche. Or maybe a hearty, rustic egg sandwich dripping with melted cheese. Whether you serve these dishes for a late breakfast or early lunch, brunch can be whatever you want to make of it, but one thing's for certain—eggs will be the star!

BREADS

French Toast
Fluffy Vanilla Pancakes
Maple Walnut Bourbon Sauce
Pancakes with Strawberries, Basil, and Cream
Pecan Pumpkin Spice Pancakes
Cardamom Streusel Blueberry Muffins
Blueberry Popovers
Pulla Bread
Bread Pudding

SANDWICHES

Grilled Cheese and Egg Sandwich
Rustic Open-Faced Egg Sandwich
Fig French Toast Sandwich
Lemony Egg Salad Sandwich with Pesto and Avocado
Basil-Walnut Pesto

BAKED EGG DISHES

Eggs in Pots
Puffy Eggs
Toasty Baked Egg Cups
Pannukakku (Finnish Oven Pancake)
Savory Cheese Soufflés
Goat Cheese Frittata with Herbs
Sweet-Potato Sausage Frittata
Classic Quiche
Tomato Caprese Quiche

FRENCH TOAST

Pulla bread is fun to make, but the one downfall is that it gets stale quickly. However, stale pulla bread makes amazing French toast! Or should I say Finnish toast? You also can use brioche or challah bread.

1 egg

1/4 cup heavy cream

1 teaspoon sugar

1 teaspoon vanilla bean paste

1/2 teaspoon grated orange peel, plus more for garnish

1/4 teaspoon ground cardamom

Pinch of salt

2 tablespoons butter, divided

Four 3/4-inch slices Pulla Bread (page 92)

Topping Options

Maple Walnut Bourbon Sauce (page 83)

Melted butter

Crème Anglaise (page 264)

Grated orange peel

Confectioners' sugar

In a shallow bowl whisk the egg, cream, sugar, vanilla bean paste, orange peel, cardamom, and salt. Melt 1 tablespoon of butter in a frying pan over medium-low heat. Once the butter melts, swirl the pan to cover the bottom evenly with butter.

While the butter is melting, dunk each slice of bread into the egg mixture, covering both sides evenly and letting the bread soak up some of the liquid, then allow any excess to drip back into the bowl. If your bread is stale, let the first batch soak in the egg while the butter is melting and let the second batch soak in the egg while the first batch cooks.

Once the butter is bubbly and foaming, add 2 soaked slices of bread to the pan and lightly brown each side, flipping the bread carefully with a spatula or pair of tongs after the first side is done. Add the remaining tablespoon of butter to the pan and cook the second batch of bread.

Arrange the French toast on two plates and drizzle with preferred topping(s).

FLUFFY VANILLA PANCAKES

When I was a little girl, my mom would push me in my stroller and take me down the road to my great-grandmother's house, for pancakes made with eggs from her chickens and cooked in a cast-iron skillet on her woodstove. Although I don't have her recipe and don't cook my pancakes on our woodstove, I love the connection I feel to my family every time I make them.

MAKES ABOUT EIGHT 4-INCH PANCAKES

2 cups all-purpose flour

4 teaspoons baking powder

2 tablespoons sugar

1/2 teaspoon kosher salt

2 eggs

1 1/2 cups milk

1 teaspoon vanilla bean paste

1/4 cup (1/2 stick) butter, melted, plus several pats more for the griddle or skillet

Topping Options

Melted butter

Confectioners' sugar

Maple syrup or Maple Walnut Bourbon Sauce (page 83)

Crème Anglaise (page 264)

In a large bowl whisk the flour, baking powder, sugar, and salt. In a small bowl whisk the eggs until they're light and frothy, then whisk in the milk, vanilla bean paste, and melted butter. Slowly add the egg mixture to the flour mixture, whisking until combined. Let the batter rest for a few minutes while you prepare the skillet.

Heat a skillet or griddle on medium and add a pat of butter. When the butter has melted and stopped bubbling, ladle about 1/4 cup of batter for each pancake into the skillet, cooking 2 or 3 pancakes at a time. Cook each pancake until bubbles form on the top around the edges, about 60 to 90 seconds.

Peek underneath each pancake to see if the bottom is golden brown and, once it is, flip the pancake and cook until the second side is golden, another 60 to 90 minutes.

Repeat with the remaining batter, adding more butter as needed to the skillet. Use a spatula to transfer pancakes to plates and serve with preferred topping(s).

FOR EVEN FLUFFIER PANCAKES

For super-fluffy pancakes, separate the 2 eggs and whisk the yolks in with the other wet ingredients. In a stand mixer with a whisk attachment, beat the whites on medium-high 5 to 6 minutes, until stiff peaks form. Combine the egg and flour mixtures, then gently fold the whites into the batter. Cook as directed.

MAPLE WALNUT BOURBON SAUCE

This decadent sauce takes only a few minutes to make, and once you've tried it poured over pancakes, you'll never go back to plain maple syrup. It's also tasty over my Vanilla Ice Cream (page 237). We're lucky here in Maine to be able to find local maple syrup, which is what you want: the real stuff. So don't scrimp on the ingredients for this recipe.

MAKES ABOUT 1 ¼ CUPS

3/4 cup maple syrup

1/4 cup (1/2 stick) butter

3 tablespoons bourbon

1/4 cup walnut halves or pieces

1 teaspoon vanilla bean paste

Pinch of kosher salt

In a small saucepan over low heat, stir together the maple syrup, butter, and bourbon. Simmer about 10 to 12 minutes and continue stirring, until the butter melts and the sauce reduces and thickens slightly. Remove the pan from the heat and stir in the walnuts and vanilla bean paste. Season with a pinch of salt. Cool slightly, then pour over pancakes or ice cream.

PANCAKES

WITH STRAWBERRIES, BASIL, AND CREAM

When strawberries and basil are in season here in Maine, I forego drizzling my pancakes with maple syrup and butter and instead whip up this special topping, which is the best of summer on a plate. Strawberries and basil are a wonderful combination, and each brings out the best in the other, like any good marriage. Don't have basil? Try mint instead. Depending on how ripe your berries are, you might not need all the sugar, so taste your strawberries as they're macerating and add sugar only as needed.

——— MAKES TOPPING FOR EIGHT 4-INCH PANCAKES ———

2 cups strawberries, hulled and
    rough chopped
1 to 2 teaspoons granulated
    sugar
Fluffy Vanilla Pancakes
    (page 82)
1/2 cup heavy cream
1 teaspoon confectioners' sugar,
    plus more for dusting
Fresh basil leaves

Put the strawberries in a medium-sized bowl, sprinkle with granulated sugar, and stir to combine.

Make the Fluffy Vanilla Pancakes as directed in the recipe.

To make whipped cream, use a stand mixer with a whisk attachment to beat the cream and confectioners' sugar on medium-high 2 to 3 minutes, until soft peaks form.

Top the pancakes with the macerated strawberries, drizzling any juice on top of the berries, then add a dollop of whipped cream, basil leaves, and confectioners' sugar.

PECAN PUMPKIN SPICE PANCAKES

I never thought of pancakes as seasonal until I had some pumpkin puree leftover after Thanksgiving and was looking for ways to use it. Instead of giving it to the chickens as I normally do, I experimented with pumpkin pancakes. I'm sorry to say that the chickens won't get any more leftover puree! These pumpkin spice pancakes are a pleasant alternative to plain pancakes and can help you usher in crisp fall day, especially with a side of Brown Sugar Maple Bacon (page 143). If you have ground pumpkin spice, feel free to use that, or create your own spice mix, as I have here.

MAKES ABOUT EIGHT 4-INCH PANCAKES

1 1/2 cups all-purpose flour

2 teaspoons baking powder

1/4 teaspoon baking soda

1 teaspoon ground cinnamon

1 teaspoon ground ginger

1/2 teaspoon ground nutmeg

1/4 teaspoon kosher salt

1 cup milk

1 egg

1/2 cup canned pumpkin puree

3 tablespoons melted butter, plus several pats for the skillet or griddle

3 tablespoons maple syrup, plus more for drizzling

1 teaspoon vanilla bean paste

1/2 cup chopped pecans, plus more for topping

In a medium-sized bowl whisk the flour, baking powder, baking soda, cinnamon, ginger, nutmeg, and salt. In a small bowl whisk the milk, egg, pumpkin, melted butter, maple syrup, and vanilla bean paste. Whisk the milk mixture into the flour mixture until combined. Stir in the pecans.

Melt a pat of butter in a large skillet or griddle over medium heat. Ladle about 1/4 cup of batter per pancake at a time into the skillet. Cook until the batter starts to puff and bubble, about 1 1/2 minutes, then flip and cook about 2 more minutes, until both sides are golden brown in the middle with crispy edges.

Repeat with the remaining batter, adding more butter as needed to the skillet. Serve warm, drizzled with maple syrup and topped with pecans.

CARDAMOM STREUSEL BLUEBERRY MUFFINS

Blueberry muffins are the quintessential breakfast treat. Wild Maine blueberries are smaller than regular high-bush berries and pack a concentrated punch of flavor. You should be able to find Maine blueberries in the freezer section of your grocery store, but if not, you can substitute regular berries. The streusel topping is optional; the muffins will be delectable either way.

MAKES 12 MUFFINS

Cardamom Blueberry Muffins

Butter for greasing the muffin tin, optional

1 3/4 cups Maine blueberries, fresh or frozen

2 cups plus 1 tablespoon all-purpose flour, divided

1 cup milk, room temperature

1 teaspoon fresh lime juice

2 1/2 teaspoons baking powder

1 teaspoon baking soda

1/2 teaspoon ground cardamom

1/4 teaspoon kosher salt

2 eggs, room temperature

1/4 cup (1/2 stick) butter, melted

1/4 cup cooking oil

1/4 cup granulated sugar

1/4 firmly packed light brown sugar

2 teaspoons vanilla bean paste

Grated peel of 1 lime, about 2 teaspoons

For the Muffins

Preheat the oven to 400 degrees. Line a standard 12- cup muffin tin with paper liners or use butter to grease the bottoms and sides of the cups. Toss the blueberries in a small bowl with 1 tablespoon of flour to coat the berries evenly. Combine the milk and lime juice in a glass measuring cup to make curdled milk.

In a small bowl whisk the remaining flour, baking powder, baking soda, cardamom, and salt. In a large mixing bowl whisk the eggs, then whisk in the butter, oil, curdled milk, granulated sugar, brown sugar, vanilla bean paste, and lime peel until smooth. Whisk the flour mixture into the egg mixture until combined. With a wooden spoon or rubber spatula, gently fold in the flour-coated blueberries.

Using a #16 disher-style ice cream scoop or spoon, divide the batter among the muffin cups, filling each with about 1/4 cup of batter or until nearly full.

Streusel Topping

⅓ cup all-purpose flour

⅓ cup sugar

3 tablespoons butter, room
  temperature

⅛ teaspoon ground cardamom

Pinch of kosher salt

For the Streusel Topping

Mash the flour, sugar, butter, cardamom, and salt in a small bowl with a fork until combined and crumbly, then sprinkle over the tops of the muffins, pressing slightly to adhere.

Bake about 18 to 20 minutes, until the tops are lightly browned and spring back when you press on them and when a toothpick inserted in the center comes out clean. Cool the muffins in the pan on a wire rack for 5 minutes, then remove the muffins from the pan and cool them further on the rack. Serve warm or at room temperature. Store leftovers loosely covered at room temperature for 3 to 4 days or freeze for longer storage.

BLUEBERRY POPOVERS

Popovers are fun to make and a tasty alternative to dinner rolls or bread. I adore these Blueberry Popovers served with blueberry jam sauce and blueberry butter and garnished with fresh mint. Both the jam and butter can be made in advance and refrigerated until you're ready to serve your popovers, or you can prepare the toppings while the popovers are baking. If you have a popover pan, use that. If not, a muffin tin will do.

MAKES 12 POPOVERS

Popovers

4 eggs, room temperature
1 cup milk, room temperature
1 cup all-purpose flour
1 teaspoon kosher salt
2 tablespoons butter
Fresh mint for garnish
Confectioners' sugar for garnish

For the Popovers

In a medium-sized bowl whisk the eggs and milk, then whisk in the flour and salt. The batter will be thin like pancake batter. Pour the batter into a 2-cup measuring cup and let sit for at least 30 minutes (or overnight in the fridge). If you are using chilled batter, let it sit for 30 minutes to come to room temperature, then give it a good whisk before pouring it into the pan.

Preheat the oven to 425 degrees and set the rack in the bottom third section of the oven.

Cut the butter into 12 cubes and put 1 cube into the bottom of each of the popover or muffin cups. Then set the pan in the oven as it preheats and melt the butter for a few minutes while the batter rests. Once the butter has melted, remove the tin from the oven, brush the sides of each muffin cup with the butter, and fill each cup about halfway with the batter.

The popover effect is a result of steam, so be sure to keep the oven closed until the popovers have baked a full 30 minutes. If you open the oven, they're likely to collapse. Bake for 15 minutes, then reduce the heat to 350 degrees and bake for another 15 minutes. Then check on them through the oven window and bake for another few minutes, if necessary, until they're puffed and golden brown. While the popovers are baking, prepare the jam sauce. Remove the pan from the oven and cool on a wire rack.

Blueberry Jam Sauce

1 cup fresh or frozen
  blueberries
1/4 cup sugar
Grated peel of half a lime,
  about 1 teaspoon

Blueberry Butter

1/2 cup (1 stick) butter, room
  temperature, sliced into
  tablespoons
3 tablespoons warm Blueberry
  Jam Sauce

For the Blueberry Jam Sauce

Combine the blueberries, sugar, and grated lime peel in a saucepan over medium heat and cook, stirring occasionally, until the mixture becomes thick and jammy, about 10 to 15 minutes. Remove the pan from the heat to cool. While the sauce is still cooling, measure out 3 tablespoons for the Blueberry Butter.

For the Blueberry Butter

Put the butter slices in a small bowl. Mash the warm Blueberry Jam Sauce into the butter with a fork until well combined. Spoon the butter onto a sheet of wax paper and roll the butter into a 1-inch log. Chill the butter until you're ready to serve the popovers, then cut the log into 12 even slices.

Place a popover on a dessert plate and serve with a dollop of Blueberry Jam Sauce on the side, a slice of Blueberry Butter, fresh mint, and a dusting of confectioners' sugar.

PULLA BREAD

I look forward to fall each year because it means we start lighting our woodstove. It also means it's time to bake bread again, letting it rise in front of the fire. Pulla bread is always the first loaf I make to kick off the season. The heady scents of yeast and cardamom drift through the house, reminding me of when I'd help my mom make this Finnish braided bread. Pulla is a sweet yeast bread similar to Jewish challah or French brioche, although the cardamom flavoring and coarse Swedish pearl sugar on top set pulla bread apart, making it solidly Scandinavian. It gets stale quickly, so it's best to eat it right away—or save some to make bread pudding or French toast.

MAKES 1 LOAF

3 1/4 cups all-purpose flour

2 1/2 teaspoons ground cardamom, divided

1/2 teaspoon kosher salt

3 eggs, divided

2/3 cup milk

1/3 cup granulated sugar

3 tablespoons butter, cut into cubes, plus more for the bowl

2 1/4 teaspoons active dry yeast

1 teaspoon heavy cream

2 teaspoons Swedish pearl sugar

In a medium-sized bowl whisk the flour, 2 teaspoons of the cardamom, and salt.

In a small bowl whisk 2 of the eggs. In a small saucepan over medium-low heat, combine the milk and granulated sugar using a whisk, then add the butter. Continue to whisk until the butter is melted, then remove the pan from the heat and let it cool to around 100 to 110 degrees (cooling below 120 degrees will prevent the yeast from dying). Whisk in the yeast and let the mixture sit for 10 minutes until the top foams and starts to bubble.

Pour the yeast mixture into a stand mixer with a dough hook. Add the whisked eggs and mix on low to combine. Add the flour mixture, 1/2 cup at a time, and combine on low 1 to 2 minutes until all the flour is incorporated. Scrape down the sides of the bowl with a rubber spatula as needed. Once the dough forms a cohesive ball, increase the mixer speed to medium and knead 10 to 12 more minutes, until the dough is glossy and smooth, not sticky. Alternatively, you can hand-knead the dough.

Lightly butter a large mixing bowl and transfer the dough to it. Cover the bowl with a clean, damp kitchen towel or plastic wrap and set it in a warm spot for about 1 hour, or until the dough almost doubles in size. (If your house is cold, trying setting the bowl in front of the woodstove or in a beam of sunshine streaming through a window.) Punch the dough down, replace the towel or plastic wrap, and let the dough continue rising for 30 minutes.

Preheat the oven to 375 degrees and line a rimmed baking sheet with parchment paper.

Punch the dough down again, then using a bench scraper, divide it into 3 equal balls and let the dough rest for 10 minutes on a floured surface. Then stretch each ball into a 15-inch rope. Lay the ropes side by side and braid them together, pinching each end to secure the braid. Place the loaf on the prepared baking sheet, tuck the ends of the loaf under, then let the dough rise for another 30 minutes.

Once the dough has finished rising, whisk the remaining egg with the heavy cream and remaining $1/2$ teaspoon of cardamom. Generously brush the loaf with the mixture, making sure to get it into all the nooks and crannies. Sprinkle with the pearl sugar and bake on the center oven rack for 25 to 30 minutes until the crust is golden brown. Cool the loaf on a wire rack, then slice and serve.

Leftovers can be wrapped tightly and stored on the counter for a day or so. Reheat by wrapping the loaf in aluminum foil and setting it in a warm oven for several minutes.

EASTER EGG BRAID

For a fun pulla bread variation, tuck 4 or 5 clean, raw eggs into the braid. Brush the eggs lightly with vegetable oil and bake as directed. The eggs cook as the bread bakes. Use colored eggs from your chickens or eggs dyed with natural plant dyes to make an Easter egg bread.

BREAD PUDDING

Bread pudding can not only help you use up eggs but also random pieces of stale bread. It's a versatile comfort food, adaptable to add-ins such as chocolate chips, dried or fresh fruit, or different spices. A sweet bread like challah, brioche, or pulla is best, and homemade bread is better, but you can use any bread or rolls. The bread should be slightly hard, so if it's not stale, leave it out overnight or pop the cubes into the oven for a few minutes while it's preheating.

MAKES 6 TO 8 SERVINGS

5 to 6 generous cups bread, cut
   into 1-inch cubes
2 cups milk
1/3 cup sugar
1/4 cup (1/2 stick) butter, plus
   more for greasing pan
1/2 teaspoon ground cardamom
Pinch of kosher salt
1 teaspoon vanilla bean paste
2 eggs

Topping Options
Confectioners' sugar
Crème Anglaise (page 264)
Maple Walnut Bourbon Sauce
   (page 83)
Whipped cream
Fresh berries

Butter an 8- or 9-inch square baking dish and spread the cubed bread evenly in the dish.

In a small saucepan over low heat, combine the milk, sugar, butter, cardamon, and salt. Continue stirring until the butter melts. Remove the pan from the heat, stir in the vanilla bean paste, and cool while the oven heats.

Preheat the oven to 350 degrees.

Once the milk mixture has cooled, lightly whisk in the eggs, then pour the liquid over the bread. Make sure the bread is submerged, then let it sit for 30 minutes to absorb some of the liquid.

Bake about 35 to 40 minutes, until the tips of the bread are a crusty golden brown and the middle of the custard is set. Serve warm or at room temperature topped with confectioners' sugar, Crème Anglaise or Maple Walnut Bourbon Sauce, whipped cream, or fresh berries.

Refrigerate leftovers and eat within 2 to 3 days.

GRILLED CHEESE AND EGG SANDWICH

Can't decide if you want a fried egg sandwich or a grilled cheese sandwich? Why not have both? I love to experiment with different combinations of cheeses, so go wild! Try combinations like Swiss and Gouda or Havarti and Cheddar. And if you're feeling especially adventurous, slather the bread with Basil-Walnut Pesto (page 101) before you add the cheese.

MAKES 2 SANDWICHES

2 to 3 tablespoons butter, divided

4 eggs, divided

Kosher salt

Freshly ground black pepper

4 slices bread, divided

4 slices cheese, divided

Melt 1 tablespoon of butter in a large skillet over low heat. Fry 2 eggs over easy or over hard, depending on your preference. Season with salt and pepper. Then stack one egg on top of the other along the side of the skillet. Melt another tablespoon of butter in the skillet.

Place 2 slices of bread in the skillet, top each with a slice of cheese, then add a fried egg. Cook on low heat until the cheese melts and the bread is golden brown. Then flip 1 bread/cheese/egg slice onto the other, remove from the skillet, and cut the sandwich in half. Repeat with the remaining bread, eggs, and cheese, adding more butter if necessary.

RUSTIC OPEN-FACED EGG SANDWICH

A good friend of mine who lives on the West Coast inspired this recipe. He's a stay-at-home dad with two toddlers, so he grabs food when he can. And what he grabs must be filling and nutritious, as well as delicious. These Rustic Open-Faced Egg Sandwiches fit the bill not only for lunch but also for a quick breakfast or a light dinner. Homemade sourdough bread makes the best sandwich in my opinion, but any crusty, chewy bread works. Cut a thick slice to make your sandwich easier to eat. As for the cheese, that's your call. I've found that Monterey Jack or Cheddar works well.

MAKES 2 SANDWICHES

Butter or oil, for frying

2 eggs

2 slices bread

Mayonnaise

Handful of fresh spinach

4 slices crispy cooked bacon

2 slices Cheddar cheese

Kosher salt

Freshly ground black pepper

Fry the eggs to taste. Toast the bread slices, then slather with mayonnaise. Lay the spinach on each slice of bread, then top with bacon, cheese, and a fried egg. Season with salt and pepper.

FIG FRENCH TOAST SANDWICH

I discovered this recipe when our refrigerator was fairly empty, and I was trying to find something to make for lunch. I wanted a grilled cheese sandwich, but in a cruel twist of fate, we had no cheese or butter. But we did have half a package of cream cheese and a jar of fig jam, which became part of the most luscious French toast sandwich you could imagine. It's now a standard even when we do have butter and cheese!

MAKES 2 SANDWICHES

4 ounces cream cheese, room
  temperature
4 slices bread
1 tablespoon fig jam
2 eggs
1 tablespoon milk
2 tablespoons walnut oil

Spread half of the cream cheese on 2 slices of bread. Spread the fig jam on top, dividing it between the bread slices. Spread the remaining cream cheese on the other 2 bread slices. Place them cream-cheese side down on top of the fig jam to make 2 sandwiches.

In a shallow bowl whisk the eggs and milk. Heat the oil in a large skillet on medium. Dip both sides of the sandwiches into the egg mixture, covering the sides evenly and allowing any excess liquid to drip back into the bowl. Cook the sandwiches until they're golden brown, 2 to 3 minutes on each side. Slice each sandwich in half and serve.

LEMONY EGG SALAD SANDWICH

WITH PESTO AND AVOCADO

Egg salad and egg salad sandwiches are a quintessential summertime lunch. You can stick with the basics and squash your egg salad between two slices of bread or add some avocado and pesto to my recipe. For a buttery, crispy egg salad, chop a few fried eggs into chunks and use them in this recipe.

MAKES 2 SANDWICHES

4 hard-cooked eggs, cooled and
   peeled (page 23)
1/4 cup mayonnaise
Grated peel of half a lemon
   (about 1/2 tablespoon), plus
   more for garnish
Juice of half a lemon (about
   1 1/2 tablespoons)
1/4 cup diced celery
1 tablespoon sliced scallions
1 teaspoon chopped fresh dill
Kosher salt
White pepper
4 slices bread
2 tablespoons Basil-Walnut
   Pesto (page 101)
1/2 avocado, sliced
Leafy greens (such as spinach,
   lettuce, chard, or nasturtium)

In a medium-sized bowl mash the eggs into chunks using a fork or pastry blender. Stir in the mayonnaise, grated lemon peel, lemon juice, celery, scallions, and dill. Season with salt and pepper.

Spread 2 slices of the bread with some pesto, then top with a few slices of avocado and a leafy green. Pile high with the egg salad, then top off your sandwiches with the other slices of bread.

BASIL-WALNUT PESTO

Standard pesto uses pine nuts, which I usually don't have on hand, so I use walnuts. If you can find walnut oil, use that for an extra kick of nutty goodness; otherwise go with olive oil, which the classic recipe calls for. With pesto, you can use almost any herb and oil combination. It's forgiving that way. And it's a fantastic addition to scrambled or fried eggs, egg sandwiches, and pasta dishes, or stirred into mayonnaise.

MAKES ABOUT 2 CUPS

2 cups fresh basil

3 to 4 garlic cloves

1/2 cup walnuts

1/2 to 3/4 cup walnut oil or extra-virgin olive oil

1/2 cup freshly grated Parmesan cheese

1/8 teaspoon kosher salt, plus more to taste

Freshly ground black pepper

In a food processor, pulse the basil, garlic, and walnuts several times to combine. Slowly drizzle in 1/2 cup of the oil. Add the Parmesan and salt and pulse until your pesto is smooth and the consistency you want, adding more oil if desired to thin your pesto. Then season with salt and pepper.

Use immediately or press a piece of plastic wrap over the surface, to prevent discoloring on the top, and refrigerate leftovers. Use the pesto within 3 to 5 days or freeze it in ice cube trays and store for several months.

EGGS IN POTS

Eggs in Pots, or *oeufs en cocotte*, is a French method of baking eggs slowly in individual dishes or "cocottes." The fresh butter and heavy cream in this recipe enhance the richness of the eggs. With the easy preparation and sophisticated presentation, it's a wonderful way to prepare eggs for a large group. If you're having guests over for brunch, you can double or triple the recipe. Many variations use herbs, cheeses, and meats in the ramekins, but I keep it simple with some fresh tarragon and a hint of nutmeg, both of which pair well with eggs.

MAKES 4 SERVINGS

Butter for greasing the
   ramekins
1/2 cup heavy cream
1/4 teaspoon ground nutmeg,
   plus more for seasoning
Kosher salt
White pepper
1/4 cup chopped fresh tarragon,
   plus more for garnish
4 eggs

Preheat the oven to 325 degrees. Use butter to generously grease the inside of four 4- to 6-ounce ramekins or cocottes. Set a kettle of water on the stove and bring to a boil.

Whisk the cream, nutmeg, salt, and pepper in a small bowl. Into each ramekin, pour 1 tablespoon of the cream mixture (enough to cover the bottom) and evenly distribute the tarragon. Then crack an egg gently onto the cream, taking care not to break the yolk. Divide the remaining cream among the ramekins, pouring it over each egg. Season with salt, pepper, and nutmeg.

Set the ramekins in a roasting pan or casserole dish and pour boiling water into the dish so it comes halfway up the sides of the ramekins. Bake 14 to 15 minutes until the egg whites are set and the yolks are still runny. For a firmer yolk, bake another 2 to 3 minutes. Carefully remove the ramekins from the water bath, garnish with tarragon, and serve warm.

PUFFY EGGS

If you're the type of person who always has some puff pastry tucked away in the freezer, these puffy eggs—baked eggs surrounded by a flaky crust—are a super-easy, fun way to mix up your breakfast routine. The tarragon adds a unique flavor, but if it's not your thing, you can substitute chopped chives, parsley, or dill.

MAKES 8 SERVINGS

9 eggs, divided

1 tablespoon heavy cream

1 sheet frozen puff pastry, thawed

All-purpose flour for dusting

Kosher salt

Freshly ground black pepper

2 tablespoons chopped fresh tarragon for garnish

Line a rimmed baking sheet with parchment paper. In a small bowl whisk 1 egg with the heavy cream. Then lay the sheet of puff pastry on a floured surface and cut out 4 circles with a 3-inch cookie cutter, biscuit cutter, or the rim of a medium-sized drinking glass. Use a rolling pin to roll out 4-inch circles. Gather the pastry scraps, roll them out, and repeat so you have eight 4-inch circles. Use the cookie cutter to score a smaller 3-inch circle in the center of each pastry, leaving a 1/2-inch border around the edge.

Place the circles, spaced evenly apart, on the prepared baking sheet. Prick the centers with a fork, then chill the circles for 15 minutes. Preheat the oven to 400 degrees.

Once the pastry is chilled, brush each circle with some of the whisked egg mixture. Bake until the edges start to rise and barely turn brown, about 7 to 8 minutes.

Remove the pastry from the oven, reprick each circle to deflate the centers, and if necessary create a depression in the middle with the back of a spoon to make a nest for the egg. Carefully crack 1 egg into the center of each circle, making sure not to break the yolk or let the white flow over the raised edge. Season with salt and pepper and return the pastry to the oven. Bake for another 9 to 10 minutes, until the egg whites are fully cooked, the yolks are slightly set, and the pastry is golden brown.

Remove the pastries from the oven, top them with the chopped tarragon, and serve.

TOASTY BAKED EGG CUPS

If you're like me and enjoy eating breakfast with one hand, while using the other hand to type or scroll through your social media feed, these egg cups are for you! Eggs, cheese, and crunchy toast combine in muffin tins for a compact, convenient bite. I usually don't add meat, but if you wish, you could crumble some cooked sausage or bacon in the cups before you add the cheese. These are also easy to make for a crowd because they bake up a dozen at a time and look a lot fancier than they are! I like Gouda or Cheddar cheese in my egg cups, but feel free to experiment.

MAKES 12 SERVINGS

12 slices sandwich bread
6 tablespoons butter, melted
3/4 cup shredded Gouda cheese
12 eggs
Kosher salt
Freshly ground black pepper
Chopped chives for garnish

Preheat the oven to 375 degrees. Trim the crusts off the bread slices and use a rolling pin to flatten each slice into a square. (Save the trimmings to make Bread Pudding [page 94] or Toasty Holiday Strata [page 170].)

Generously brush both sides of each slice of bread with the melted butter and then press 1 slice into each cup of a standard muffin tin, forming bread "bowls." Divide the cheese among the cups, then carefully break and slide 1 egg into each cup. Season with salt and pepper.

Bake the egg cups about 17 minutes until the whites are set, the yolks are cooked to your liking, and the toast points are golden brown. Remove the pan from the oven and run the tip of a butter knife around the edge of each cup to loosen it from the pan.

Let the toast cups cool for a few minutes, then carefully remove them from the pan (2 forks make this easier). Garnish with chopped chives and serve.

PANNUKAKKU (FINNISH OVEN PANCAKE)

A cross between a popover and a Yorkshire pudding, Pannukakku is the Finnish version of a Dutch Baby. Both my mother and grandmother used to bake this dish, so it's a childhood treat I remember fondly. The custardy batter, scented with hints of cardamom, is baked in the oven until it puffs up, and it can be savory or sweet, depending on the topping. It's slightly sweet on its own but pairs well with bacon, sausage links, or herbs like tarragon or dill. Pannukakku is often baked in a square pan, but I use a cast-iron skillet. Leftovers can be refrigerated and reheated or eaten at room temperature.

MAKES 8 SERVINGS

6 eggs

1 1/2 cups milk

2 tablespoons sugar

1 teaspoon vanilla bean paste

1 1/2 cups all-purpose flour

1 teaspoon baking powder

1/8 teaspoon ground cardamom

1/2 teaspoon salt

1/4 cup (1/2 stick) butter

Topping Options

Confectioners' sugar for dusting

Jam

Fresh fruit

In a large bowl whisk the eggs, milk, sugar, and vanilla bean paste. In a medium-sized bowl whisk the flour, baking powder, cardamom, and salt. Add the flour mixture to the egg mixture and whisk until smooth and no lumps remain. The batter will be thin and look like pancake batter.

Let the batter rest for 10 to 15 minutes while you preheat the oven to 425 degrees. Add butter to a 10-inch cast-iron skillet and put it in the oven for a few minutes or until the butter melts. Swirl the pan to evenly cover the bottom with butter.

Once the batter has rested, pour it into the hot skillet and bake until your Pannukakku is puffy and golden brown, about 12 to 15 minutes. Remove the pan from the oven and let it cool for a few minutes, then cut the Pannukakku into slices or wedges and serve topped with confectioners' sugar, jam, or fresh fruit.

SAVORY CHEESE SOUFFLÉS

Although the thought of making a soufflé might intimidate you, I find these individual soufflés easier to make than a large one. And what's the worst that could happen? If your soufflé collapses, it will still taste divine. Once you've mastered the technique and made the perfect soufflé, you'll feel a sense of satisfaction. This is my standby recipe for a basic savory soufflé, with Parmesan cheese. If you've made it correctly, it should be light and fluffy and practically melt in your mouth.

MAKES 6 SINGLE-SERVING SOUFFLÉS

Butter and cornmeal for
   prepping the ramekins
6 eggs, room temperature,
   divided
1 cup milk
$1/4$ cup heavy cream
Fresh thyme sprig
2 tablespoons butter
$1/4$ cup all-purpose flour
3 tablespoons sherry
$1/4$ cup freshly grated Parmesan
   cheese
$1/2$ teaspoon sea salt
Freshly ground nutmeg
$1/2$ teaspoon cream of tartar

Preheat the oven to 375 degrees with the rack in the bottom third of the oven. Butter six 8-ounce ramekins and dust with cornmeal. Separate the eggs and place 3 yolks in a bowl and the 6 whites in another bowl. Save the remaining 3 yolks for another recipe.

Bring the milk, cream, and thyme to a simmer in a small saucepan over medium-low heat, stirring occasionally until the milk foams and begins to bubble. Remove the pan from the heat.

Melt the butter in a medium-sized skillet over medium heat, then sprinkle in the flour, whisking constantly until the mixture thickens, about 1 minute.

Slowly add the warm milk mixture to the skillet and whisk continuously for about 2 minutes, until the sauce is bubbling and smooth and begins to thicken.

Remove the thyme sprig and pour the liquid into a large mixing bowl. Whisk in the sherry, Parmesan cheese, salt, and nutmeg.

Whisk the egg yolks, then ladle about $1/4$ cup of the cheese mixture into the yolks. Whisk to combine, then whisk the yolk mixture into the cheese mixture. Let cool while you whisk the egg whites.

Use a stand mixer with a whisk attachment to beat the egg whites and cream of tartar on medium 35 to 45 seconds, until foamy. Increase the mixer speed to medium-high and beat 2 to 3 minutes more, until soft peaks form. The whites should still be glossy, not dry. With a wooden spoon or rubber spatula, fold one-third of the egg whites into the cheese mixture, then carefully fold in the remaining egg whites until combined.

Ladle the mixture into the prepared ramekins, filling each to within $1/4$ inch of the top rim. Gently smooth the top of the soufflé batter with a rubber spatula and run your thumb around the inside rim of each ramekin to remove any drips. Place the ramekins on a rimmed baking sheet.

Bake the soufflés 16 to 18 minutes, until puffed and golden on top. Don't open the oven until the soufflés have been baking at least 16 minutes, or they may fall. Serve immediately.

Note: For a higher-rising soufflé, you can make a collar out of parchment that fits around the inside top rim of the ramekin. Slide it between the egg and ramekin before putting the soufflés in the oven. This gives the soufflés some extra support as they rise.

GOAT CHEESE FRITTATA
WITH HERBS

Frittata is a fancy way of saying "quiche without the crust." Frittatas are great to make when you're feeling lazy and have a lot of eggs and an assortment of vegetables or other fillings. I look forward to making this each spring when I have various fresh herbs growing in the garden. Dill, tarragon, basil, parsley, sage, and thyme are all wonderful in this dish. I love the pungent flavor of the goat cheese mingling with the fresh herbs (if you're not a goat cheese fan, you can substitute cream cheese). To me, this frittata screams, "Spring!"

MAKES 4 TO 6 SERVINGS

8 eggs

2 tablespoons heavy cream

2 teaspoons chopped chives

1/2 cup chopped mixed fresh
herbs, plus more for garnish

1/2 teaspoon kosher salt

1/8 teaspoon white pepper

1 tablespoon extra-virgin olive
oil, plus more for drizzling

4 ounces goat cheese, crumbled

Preheat the broiler (if your broiler has different settings, set it to high). In a medium-sized bowl, whisk the eggs, cream, chives, mixed herbs, salt, and pepper. Heat the oil in a medium-sized skillet or frying pan over medium heat. When the oil is shimmering, pour the egg mixture into the pan and cook for 3 to 4 minutes, lifting the edges with a spatula to let the uncooked egg seep underneath. When the edges begin to set, remove the skillet from the heat.

Sprinkle the goat cheese on top of the eggs. Broil the eggs about 3 to 4 minutes, until the center is set and the frittata is puffed and brown around the edges. Watch closely, as broiler temperatures can vary. Allow the frittata to cool for a few minutes, then cut it into wedges. Drizzle with olive oil and garnish with herbs, if desired.

SWEET-POTATO SAUSAGE FRITTATA

Frittatas are so versatile that you can add almost any combination of meats, veggies, and cheese, but I like this combination in particular. The sweet potatoes and sausage make this hearty dish an obvious choice for when you crave breakfast for dinner. A mild cheese like Fontina, Gouda, or Gruyère pairs well with the other flavors, letting the fresh sage shine through. This recipe requires a time commitment, but the roasted sweet potato and caramelized onions alone are worth the wait.

MAKES 6 TO 8 SERVINGS

1 large sweet potato, peeled and cut into $1/4$-inch rounds

2 tablespoons extra-virgin olive oil, divided

Kosher salt

Freshly ground black pepper

8 ounces uncooked sweet Italian sausage

$1/2$ sweet onion, sliced thinly

$1/4$ cup julienned fresh sage, plus whole, fresh sage for garnish

12 eggs

$1/2$ cup heavy cream

1 cup shredded Fontina cheese

Preheat the oven to 400 degrees.

In a medium-sized bowl toss the sweet potato rounds with 1 tablespoon of the olive oil and arrange them in a single layer on a rimmed baking sheet. Season the rounds with salt and pepper. Roast for 15 to 20 minutes, turning them over halfway through. When the rounds have softened and are starting to brown, remove the baking sheet from the oven and cool slightly.

While the sweet potato rounds are roasting, heat the remaining tablespoon of olive oil in an oven-safe skillet on medium-low. Add the sausage, breaking up any large chunks, and cook until lightly browned and no longer pink. Remove the sausage from the pan, draining all but 1 teaspoon of the grease, and add the onions. Season with salt and pepper. Cook the onions, stirring occasionally, until golden brown and caramelized, about 30 minutes. Return the sweet potato rounds and the sausage to the skillet and top with the julienned sage.

Whisk the eggs, cream, and cheese in a large bowl and season with salt and pepper. Pour over the top of the sausage-and-vegetable mixture in the skillet. Bake 20 to 25 minutes until the egg is lightly browned, puffed, and set. Slice the frittata into wedges and serve warm or at room temperature with a garnish of fresh sage.

CLASSIC QUICHE

I don't make quiche often because it's more time consuming than making a frittata, which is similar but doesn't require a crust. However, any time I do make the effort, I'm reminded that the process isn't that difficult.

You can customize this basic recipe with more cheese or with vegetables. Quiche can be served slightly warm or at room temperature.

MAKES 6 TO 8 SERVINGS

Basic Pastry Crust

1 1/4 cups all-purpose flour

1/4 teaspoon kosher salt

1/2 cup (1 stick) cold butter, cut into tablespoons

1 egg yolk

2 tablespoons ice water

Quiche Filling

5 eggs

1/2 cup heavy cream

1/2 cup milk

1/2 cup grated Parmesan cheese

Kosher salt

White pepper

For the Crust

In a medium-sized bowl, stir together the flour and salt. Add the butter and mix with a pastry blender or fork until the butter pieces are about pea-size. Add the egg yolk and mix until combined. Gradually pour in the ice water, mixing until the dough forms but isn't wet. Wrap the dough in plastic, flatten using a roller, and chill in the refrigerator for at least 1 hour.

On a lightly floured surface, roll out the dough into a 12-inch circle. Carefully transfer it to a 9-inch tart pan with a removable bottom. Gently press the dough into the bottom of the pan and up the sides. Trim off any excess dough around the edge of the pan. Chill the dough for 30 minutes. While it is chilling, preheat the oven to 375 degrees.

Cover the dough with aluminum foil, add pie weights or dried beans on top, then bake for 15 minutes. Remove the weights and the aluminum foil, prick the crust all over with a fork, and bake for 5 more minutes, until the crust is lightly browned. Remove from the oven and reduce the oven temperature to 325 degrees.

For the Filling

While the oven is cooling, prepare the filling. In a medium-sized bowl whisk the eggs, cream, and milk. Stir in the Parmesan cheese. Season with salt and pepper.

Once the oven temperature cools to 325 degrees, pour the filling into the prepared crust.

Bake about 30 minutes, until the quiche is set and lightly browned around the edges. Tent the quiche with aluminum foil if the crust begins to brown too quickly. Remove the quiche from the oven and allow it to cool for 10 to 20 minutes, or to room temperature. Remove the sides of the tart pan and slice the quiche into wedges to serve.

Note: Instead of cream and milk, you can use 1 cup of half-and-half.

TOMATO CAPRESE QUICHE

When our summer garden is bursting with tomatoes and fresh basil, I could eat a caprese salad every day! For this recipe, I borrow all the flavors of a caprese salad and add eggs. This quiche should only be made when you can locally source the freshest, juiciest, vine-ripened tomatoes. Fresh eggs and basil also are a must. Cut this dense, savory quiche into slices and eat it almost like a pizza.

MAKES 6 TO 8 SERVINGS

Basic Pastry Crust (page 116)

Tomato Caprese Quiche Filling

1 tablespoon butter

1/4 cup diced shallot

3 garlic cloves, minced

Kosher salt

Freshly ground black pepper

5 eggs

1/2 cup heavy cream

1/2 cup grated Parmesan cheese

1/4 cup roughly chopped fresh
   basil, plus several whole
   leaves for garnish

2 Roma tomatoes, cut into
   14-inch slices

1 ball fresh mozzarella cheese,
   cut into 1/4-inch slices

Extra-virgin olive oil for
   drizzling

Balsamic vinegar for drizzling,
   optional

Make the crust as instructed in the Classic Quiche recipe (page 116). While the crust bakes, prepare the filling.

Melt the butter in a skillet over medium heat, then add the shallot and garlic and cook about 2 to 3 minutes, until softened, aromatic, and starting to brown. Season with salt and pepper.

In a medium-sized bowl whisk the eggs and cream. Stir in the Parmesan cheese, chopped basil, and the shallot mixture. Season with salt and pepper.

Once the oven temperature cools to 325 degrees, pour the filling into the prepared crust. Top with the tomato and mozzarella slices.

Bake for about 30 minutes, until the quiche is set and lightly browned around the edges. Tent the quiche with aluminum foil if the crust begins to brown too quickly. Remove the quiche from the oven and allow it to cool for 10 to 20 minutes, or to room temperature. Remove the sides of the tart pan and slice the quiche into wedges. Garnish with whole basil leaves and drizzle with olive oil and balsamic vinegar, if desired.

SIPS AND NIBBLES

Enjoy while the chickens scratch in the yard

There's no place I'd rather spend my time on a warm summer afternoon after chores are done than sitting in the shade, sipping a cold beverage, and nibbling finger foods with my husband while the chickens frolic in the grass. Eggs are the ultimate bite-size snack all by themselves, but let's get creative. In this chapter, eggs are front and center in a handful of snacks, as well as some thirst-quenching beverages, to enjoy from sunrise to sunset. "Happy hours" are truly that: hours whiled away winding down and relaxing at the end of the day watching the chickens wander. If you keep the glasses full and serve enough nibbles, cocktail hour may end up negating the need for dinner.

SIPS

Egg Flip

Lime Bourbon Sour

Maple Sour

Sunny-Side Up Sidecar

Boozy Spiced Eggnog

NIBBLES

Deviled Eggs with Avocado Oil and Sage

Deviled Eggs with Turmeric

Gruyère Gougères

Maple Bacon Scotch Eggs

Broccoli Cheddar Tart

Brown Sugar Maple Bacon

Butter Crackers

Lemon-Basil Bars

EGG FLIP

The flip is a colonial cocktail that was originally made with ale and rum and served warm, but now it's loosely defined as a frothy alcoholic beverage that contains sugar and an egg. A cousin to eggnog, this satisfying cocktail whips up quickly. My version uses brandy and cardamom, but experiment with different flavor combinations. As with any cocktails calling for egg foam, dry-shaking the egg with the other ingredients in a shaker (meaning before you add the ice) will result in the foamiest topper.

MAKES 1 COCKTAIL

2 ounces brandy

1 teaspoon sugar

1 egg, room temperature

3 to 4 ice cubes, plus more for serving

Splash of heavy cream

Freshly grated cardamom

Add the brandy, sugar, and egg to a cocktail shaker. Dry-shake vigorously for at least 30 seconds, until the egg is foamy. Add the ice cubes and heavy cream and shake again to chill, then strain the liquid into a glass filled with ice. Garnish with cardamom.

LIME BOURBON SOUR

Whiskey sours made with store-bought sour mix were my drink of choice for a while in college. Then I became an adult and graduated to this more grown-up homemade version, which combines fresh lime juice with bourbon and calls for an egg white—technically making it a "Boston sour"—for a layer of lime-scented foam on top. "Egg whites in cocktails?" you say. "Oh yes," I reply with a grin. Dry-shaking an egg white in your cocktail shaker with an acid—in this case, the lime juice—before adding the ice adds a smooth, pillowy texture and a fun, foamy top.

MAKES 1 COCKTAIL

2 ounces bourbon

Juice of 1 lime (about 2 tablespoons)

1 ounce simple syrup

1 egg white, room temperature

3 to 4 ice cubes, plus more for serving

1 slice lime for garnish

1 maraschino cherry for garnish

Add the bourbon, lime juice, simple syrup, and egg white to a cocktail shaker or pint Mason jar. Dry-shake vigorously until the egg white is frothy, about 30 seconds. Add the ice cubes and shake until chilled, about 20 seconds more. Strain the liquid into a glass over ice. Garnish with the lime slice and maraschino cherry.

MAPLE SOUR

I created this maple version of a classic whiskey sour to sip in autumn, while we sit on our front porch enjoying the crisp fall air and marveling at the colorful Maine foliage. For a special presentation, use a large red maple leaf as a "coaster" for your cocktail.

MAKES 1 COCKTAIL

2 ounces bourbon

1 ounce freshly squeezed lemon juice

1 ounce maple syrup

1 egg white, room temperature

3 to 4 ice cubes, plus more for serving

Small maple leaf for garnish, optional

Large maple leaf for a coaster, optional

Add the bourbon, lemon juice, maple syrup, and egg white to a cocktail shaker or pint Mason jar. Shake vigorously until the egg white is foamed and frothy, about 30 seconds. Add the ice cubes and shake until well chilled, about 20 seconds. Strain the liquid into a glass over ice. Garnish with a small red maple leaf, if desired, and set the glass on the large leaf.

SUNNY-SIDE UP SIDECAR

A few years ago, I was sitting on a plane and catching up on some magazine reading. I saw a recipe for a cocktail that looked exactly like a sunny-side up egg sitting in the glass. I couldn't get the image out of my head, so once I returned home, I set about re-creating it. This is my version—a fresh, fun take on a classic sidecar. Any triple sec liqueur will do, but I prefer Cointreau.

MAKES 1 COCKTAIL

4 tablespoons frozen orange juice concentrate

1 ounce triple sec liqueur, plus more for the glass rim

Sugar, to coat the glass rim

1 1/2 ounces brandy

1/4 cup water

1 egg white

Defrost the orange juice concentrate in a small bowl on the counter, then stir in the triple sec liqueur. Measure out 2 tablespoons of this mixture, then return the rest to the freezer for several hours until refrozen.

Once the juice concentrate mixture has refrozen and you're ready to serve the sidebar, wet the rim of a coupe or martini glass with triple sec liqueur and then dip the rim in a plate of sugar.

Add the brandy, 2 tablespoons of thawed juice mixture, and water to a cocktail shaker and shake vigorously at least 30 seconds, until blended and well chilled. Strain the liquid into the glass.

Rinse out the shaker and dry-shake the egg white vigorously for 60 seconds, or use a stand mixer with a whisk attachment to whip the egg white on medium-high 10 to 15 seconds, until frothy.

Using a #30 disher-style ice cream scoop or spoon, scoop out a generous ball of the frozen orange juice mixture, about 2 tablespoons, and center it in the glass. Pour the egg white around the edge of the glass and serve.

BOOZY SPICED EGGNOG

Eggnog is typically made with brandy, but you can swap that out for your alcohol of choice. The spices pair well with brandy and amaretto to create the merriest sip of holiday cheer. The eggnog keeps in the refrigerator for several days, improving in taste and texture as it ages. For a family friendly version, omit the liquor. However, alcohol keeps the eggnog safe to drink longer, so nonalcoholic versions should be consumed immediately.

MAKES ABOUT 5 CUPS

2 cups whole milk

1/2 teaspoon ground cardamom

1/2 teaspoon ground nutmeg, plus more for garnish

1/2 teaspoon ground ginger

6 eggs, separated

3/4 cup sugar

1/8 teaspoon kosher salt

1 cup heavy cream

1 teaspoon vanilla bean paste

1/2 cup brandy, amaretto, bourbon, or rum (or a combination)

Cinnamon sticks for garnish

Add the milk, cardamom, nutmeg, and ginger to a medium saucepan and simmer over low heat, stirring occasionally, until bubbles form around the edges. Remove the pan from the heat.

In a large bowl whisk the egg yolks, sugar, and salt until frothy and pale yellow. Slowly add the hot milk, one ladleful at a time, to the egg mixture and whisk to combine. Adding the milk slowly keeps the eggs from curdling as they start to cook.

Pour the milk-and-egg mixture into the saucepan and cook over low heat, whisking constantly, 2 to 3 minutes, until it is thickened enough to coat the back of a spoon. Remove the pan from the heat and strain the mixture through a fine mesh strainer into a large bowl (straining is optional but will result in a smoother drink). Stir in the heavy cream and vanilla. Cool the mixture to room temperature, then stir in the brandy or amaretto. Cover the bowl and chill for several hours or overnight.

When you're ready to serve the eggnog, use a stand mixer with a whisk attachment to whip the egg whites on medium 35 to 45 seconds until foamy, then on medium-high 2 to 3 minutes, until soft peaks form, then use a wooden spoon or rubber spatula to fold the whites into the eggnog. Ladle the eggnog into glasses and garnish the glasses them with a sprinkle of nutmeg and a cinnamon stick.

DEVILED EGGS

WITH AVOCADO OIL AND SAGE

When I make deviled eggs, I always cook two extra eggs, to ensure that I have enough filling to pile each one high. You can prepare the filling by hand using a fork, but a food processor makes the smoothest and creamiest filling. This is my "fancy" deviled egg recipe, and I pipe the filling for a more elegant presentation. I also like the hint of avocado flavor in this recipe.

MAKES 12 DEVILED EGGS

8 hard-cooked eggs, cooled and
    peeled (page 23)
2 tablespoons mayonnaise
2 teaspoons avocado oil, plus
    more for drizzling
1 teaspoon champagne vinegar
Kosher salt
White pepper
Fresh sage for garnish

Slice each egg in half lengthwise. Carefully scoop out the yolks with a small spoon and place them in a food processor. Arrange 12 of the empty egg white halves on an egg tray, discarding the remaining 4 whites or using them later for egg salad or to feed to your chickens.

In the food processor, pulse the yolks until they're crumbled, then add the mayonnaise, avocado oil, and vinegar and pulse to combine. Season with salt and pepper. Continue to blend until the filling is smooth and creamy.

Fit a pastry bag with a $1/2$-inch round piping tip, then scoop the filling into the bag and pipe it into each egg white half. Garnish with white pepper, a drizzle of avocado oil, and the fresh sage. Serve the deviled eggs immediately or refrigerate and eat them within a few days.

DEVILED EGGS

WITH TURMERIC

Anybody can bring regular deviled eggs to a potluck or cookout. But it takes a special kind of person to bring these deviled eggs. I love how the turmeric turns the egg whites a vibrant yellow, which complements the brightness of the egg yolks.

MAKES 12 DEVILED EGGS

2 cups water

2 tablespoons ground turmeric, plus more for garnish

1 teaspoon sugar

1 teaspoon kosher salt, plus more for seasoning

1/2 teaspoon cider vinegar

8 hard-cooked eggs, cooled and peeled (page 23)

1/2 cup heavy cream

1 teaspoon freshly squeezed lemon juice

1 teaspoon extra-virgin olive oil

Freshly ground white pepper

Sliced scallions for garnish

Mustard seeds for garnish

In a medium-sized bowl whisk the water, turmeric, sugar, salt, and vinegar, until the sugar and salt are dissolved. Place the eggs in the bowl, making sure they are covered with water (add a little more if necessary, or use a less shallow bowl). Refrigerate 3 to 4 hours (or overnight), until the eggs are the desired shade of yellow.

Remove the eggs from the liquid and set on paper towels to dry. Then slice each egg in half lengthwise. Carefully remove the egg yolks with a small spoon and place in a medium-sized bowl. Arrange 12 of the empty egg white halves on an egg tray, discarding the remaining 4 whites or using them later for egg salad or to feed to your chickens.

Mash the yolks with a fork, then add the cream, lemon juice, and oil and mash until creamy and smooth. Season with salt and pepper.

Use a #30 disher-style ice cream scoop or spoon to mound about 2 tablespoons of the filling into each of the egg white halves. Garnish with sliced scallions, mustard seeds, and turmeric. Serve immediately or refrigerate and eat within a few days.

GRUYÈRE GOUGÈRES

Say that three times fast! These cheesy French puffs are addictive—so it's good that this recipe makes a few dozen! The basic choux dough used for this pastry is the same one you'd use to make cream puffs (page 222), profiteroles, or éclairs. The added cheese makes this a savory snack you'll want to prepare often. Gruyère cheese is commonly used in these puffs (which are often served with wine), but feel free to substitute a different cheese.

MAKES ABOUT 4 DOZEN

1/2 cup water, plus 1 tablespoon for brushing the tops

1/2 cup milk

1/2 cup (1 stick) butter, cut into 1/2-inch cubes

1/4 teaspoon kosher salt

1/8 teaspoon freshly ground black pepper

1 cup all-purpose flour

4 eggs, plus 1 yolk for brushing the tops

2 cups shredded Gruyère cheese

1/4 teaspoon freshly grated nutmeg

Preheat the oven to 450 degrees. Line 2 rimmed baking sheets with parchment.

In a medium-sized heavy saucepan, combine the water, milk, butter, salt, and pepper and bring to a boil over medium-high heat, stirring occasionally. Once the mixture is boiling, reduce the heat to medium-low, add the flour and stir continuously with a wooden spoon for about 2 minutes, until the dough starts to form a cohesive ball and pull away from the sides of the pan. It should look like mashed potatoes and smell slightly nutty.

Remove the pan from the heat and transfer the dough to a stand mixer with a paddle attachment. Let the dough cool for 2 to 3 minutes. On medium, add 1 egg at a time to the dough and beat until incorporated before adding the next. Scrape down the sides of the bowl as needed. Beat the dough on medium for several more minutes, until it's glossy and lemon colored. Add the cheese and nutmeg and mix until combined. The dough will be sticky.

Transfer the dough to a pastry bag with a 1/2-inch round piping tip. Pipe mounds of dough about 1 inch in diameter onto the parchment-covered baking sheets. Use approximately 1 tablespoon of dough for each mound and leave 2 inches between them. Whisk the remaining egg yolk with the tablespoon of water and brush the tops of each gougère.

Place the baking sheets in the oven and reduce the heat to 350 degrees. Bake 20 to 25 minutes, until the gougères are puffy and golden brown and sound hollow when you tap them. Don't open the oven until the full time has elapsed, because the gougères need steam to puff properly.

Serve your gougères warm from the oven or let them cool to room temperature. Store leftovers at room temperature or freeze them. Frozen gougères can be defrosted and briefly reheated in the oven.

MAPLE BACON SCOTCH EGGS

Several years ago, a visitor from the United Kingdom introduced me to Scotch eggs. My modified version of her recipe has become a family favorite. These handheld crunchy-sweet-savory bites are delicious to eat either warm or at room temperature.

MAKES 6 SCOTCH EGGS

1/4 cup all-purpose flour

Kosher salt

Freshly ground black pepper

2 eggs

1 cup coarse panko bread crumbs

1 pound pork sausage

4 slices bacon, chopped

2 tablespoons maple syrup, plus more for serving

1/4 teaspoon ground nutmeg

1/4 teaspoon ground cardamom

6 soft-cooked eggs, cooled and peeled (page 23)

Vegetable oil, for frying

Pour the flour onto a small plate and season with salt and pepper. In a shallow bowl whisk the eggs. Pour the flour onto a small plate and season with salt and pepper. Line up the dishes with flour first, then the whisked egg, then the bread crumbs. Add an empty plate beside the bowl of bread crumbs.

In a food processor pulse the sausage, bacon, maple syrup, nutmeg, and cardamom to combine. Divide the sausage mixture into 6 even portions.

Wet your hands well, then pat one portion of the sausage mixture into an oval-shaped patty on one hand. Roll a soft-cooked egg in the seasoned flour, then gently mold the pork around the egg, making sure to seal the seams well with your fingers. Handle the eggs carefully so you don't break the yolk. Roll the sausage ball in the seasoned flour, dip it into the whisked egg, then roll it in the bread crumbs. Place the Scotch egg on the empty plate. Repeat with the remaining soft-cooked eggs.

Heat 3 to 4 inches of oil in a heavy pot to 330 degrees. Once the oil is hot, carefully add 3 of the Scotch eggs to the oil and fry about 6 minutes, turning the eggs halfway through, until the sausage reaches an internal temperature of 160 degrees and the outside is golden brown and crispy. Using a slotted spoon or metal tongs, move the Scotch eggs to a paper-towel-lined wire rack to cool slightly. Repeat with the remaining batch of eggs.

Serve the Scotch eggs with maple syrup and refrigerate any leftovers. Reheat briefly or eat at room temperature.

BROCCOLI CHEDDAR TART

Sometimes I enjoy the challenge of rolling out a beautiful crust. For this tart, I like to use a classic pâte brisée crust, but you can substitute your own crust recipe or a store-bought crust. You can use a tart pan, a rectangular pan, or a regular pie plate. I use a 4 1/2 x 14-inch tart pan with a removable bottom because that makes the tart easy to cut into thin slices, to serve as an appetizer or "nibble." This tart works equally well for breakfast, brunch, or a light summer dinner paired with a salad.

MAKES 12 TO 14 SERVINGS

Pâte Brisée Crust

1 1/4 cups all-purpose flour

1/2 teaspoon kosher salt

1/2 cup (1 stick) butter, cut into 1/2-inch cubes and chilled

1/4 cup ice water

For the Crust

Add the flour and salt to a food processor. Add a few butter cubes at a time and pulse about 10 seconds, until the mixture forms coarse clumps. While the motor is running, slowly pour in the ice water and process until the dough starts to form a ball, about 30 seconds. You may not need all the water. Flatten the dough into a disc and wrap it in plastic wrap. Chill for 30 minutes and preheat the oven to 400 degrees.

The crust needs to be blind-baked before the filling is added so it's flaky and crisp, not soggy. Roll out the chilled dough on a floured surface and press it into a tart pan. Chill for another 30 minutes. Once chilled, prick the bottom of the dough with a fork, cover it with parchment paper or aluminum foil, and add pie weights or dried beans on top. Bake until the crust is set, about 16 to 18 minutes, then remove the weights and parchment and continue to bake another 10 to 12 minutes, until the crust is lightly browned and nearly done. Then remove the crust from the oven and let it cool slightly while you prepare the filling.

Reduce the oven temperature to 325 degrees.

Broccoli Cheddar Filling

5 eggs

1 cup heavy cream

1/4 teaspoon kosher salt

1/4 teaspoon freshly ground
   black pepper

1/4 teaspoon ground nutmeg

3/4 cup shredded Cheddar
   cheese

2 teaspoons all-purpose flour

4 uncooked breakfast sausage
   links, crumbled, with skins
   removed

1/2 cup broccoli florets, chopped
   into small pieces

1/4 cup finely chopped onion

2 garlic cloves, thinly sliced

For the Filling

While the crust is baking and cooling in the tart pan, whisk the eggs and cream in a small bowl, then season with salt, pepper, and nutmeg. In a different small bowl, toss the shredded cheese and flour.

Cook the crumbled sausage in a medium-sized skillet over medium-high heat until browned and crispy. Remove the sausage from the pan and drain on a paper-towel-lined plate. Add the broccoli, onion, and garlic to the same pan and cook over medium-high heat until crispy and browned.

Arrange the sausage and vegetables on the crust and cover with the cheese mixture. Pour the egg mixture over the top, being careful not to disturb the vegetables and cheese. Bake 20 to 30 minutes until the middle is set and the crust is golden brown. Cover the crust with aluminum foil, if necessary, to keep it from browning too quickly. Remove the tart from the oven and let it cool slightly. Remove the sides of the pan and slice the tart into 1-inch wedges. Serve warm or at room temperature.

BROWN SUGAR MAPLE BACON

What are eggs without bacon? This chewy, sticky, candied maple bacon is a satisfying stand-alone finger food or a tasty accompaniment on an egg sandwich or burger. Or try it crumbled over pancakes or a cupcake. This recipe doesn't take much longer to make than regular bacon. And if you can find a source for locally raised bacon, that's even better. Ditto for local maple syrup.

MAKES 12 SLICES

12 slices thick-sliced bacon
2/3 cup firmly packed brown sugar
1/3 cup maple syrup
Freshly ground black pepper

Preheat the oven to 350 degrees.

Line a rimmed baking sheet with aluminum foil, then set a wire cooling rack on top. Lay the bacon strips over the rack in a single layer.

Whisk the brown sugar and maple syrup in a small bowl until smooth. The mixture should be thick but still a spreadable consistency. Generously brush the sugar mixture over the tops of the bacon strips with a pastry brush. Then grind a copious amount of pepper over the slices.

Bake about 30 minutes, until the bacon is browned and crispy, and the tops are bubbling and sticky. You'll know it's ready when it smells so good in your kitchen that you can't take it anymore. Remove the bacon from the oven and allow it to cool on the rack for a few minutes. Then peel the slices off the rack and set them on a plate to cool.

Store leftovers in the refrigerator. Just kidding—there won't be any leftovers!

BUTTER CRACKERS

Make your own RITZ-style crackers using the piecrust dough and leftover egg white from the Cheesy Mushroom Pie. These crackers are an addictive nibble to pair with a cocktail or a glass of chilled wine, as you while away a lazy summer afternoon—which is what I like to do while I watch the chickens cavort in my backyard.

MAKES ABOUT 12 TO 16 CRACKERS

Cornmeal, for rolling

Excess Cheesy Mushroom Pie crust dough (page 176)

1 egg white

Kosher salt

Preheat the oven to 400 degrees.

On a clean surface dusted with cornmeal, roll out the excess piecrust dough to a 1/8-inch thickness. Use a 1 1/2- or 2-inch cookie or biscuit cutter, or the rim of a shot glass, to cut out dough rounds. Re-roll the scraps and cut out more rounds. Arrange the rounds, evenly spaced, on a rimmed baking sheet.

Whisk the egg white in a small bowl, then brush the tops of the crackers with the white. Prick holes in each cracker with the tines of a fork and sprinkle with kosher salt. Bake until the crackers are slightly barely browned, 8 to 10 minutes.

LEMON–BASIL BARS

These lemon-basil bars pack a citrusy punch and are super-easy to make. I love the tart sweetness of the lemon filling mingling with the savory basil. When cut into small bars, these bars can accompany a cold beverage on a warm summer day when you want something sweet.

MAKES ABOUT 36 BARS

Crust

10 tablespoons butter, room temperature

1/2 cup firmly packed light brown sugar

Grated peel of 1 lemon (about 1 tablespoon)

1 tablespoon freshly minced basil, plus more for garnish

2 cups all-purpose flour

Filling

1/2 cup all-purpose flour

6 eggs

2 cups sugar

Grated peel of 3 lemons (about 3 tablespoons), divided

Juice of 4 lemons (about 3/4 cup)

3/4 teaspoon baking powder

Confectioners' sugar for garnish

For the Crust

Preheat the oven to 350 degrees. Line a 9 x 13-inch baking pan with parchment paper, making sure excess paper hangs over the long sides of the pan.

Use a stand mixer with a paddle attachment to beat the butter, brown sugar, lemon peel, and basil on medium 1 to 2 minutes, until smooth. With the mixer set to low, slowly add the flour until the mixture is crumbly and well combined. Press the crust into the prepared pan and bake about 20 minutes, until lightly browned.

For the Filling

While the crust is baking, use a stand mixer with a paddle attachment to beat the flour, eggs, sugar, 1 tablespoon of lemon peel, lemon juice, and baking powder 1 to 2 minutes, until combined and frothy.

Pour the filling over the hot crust, return to the oven, and bake about 20 minutes, until the center of the filling is set and the edges of the crust are light brown.

Cool on a wire rack in the pan for at least an hour, then lift the bars out of the pan using the parchment paper. Cut into 1 x 3-inch bars, dust with confectioners' sugar, and garnish with fresh basil and remaining lemon peel. Cover leftovers and store them covered in the refrigerator.

DINNER

*After the evening chores are done and
the chickens have gone to roost*

I'll happily eat bacon and eggs any time of the day (and often do when our egg basket is over-flowing!), so it was hard to separate many of the recipes in this book into strict "breakfast," "brunch," and "dinner" categories. But this collection of egg recipes represents more hearty fare, such as custardy macaroni and cheese or comforting egg drop soup, suitable for after the evening chores are done. However, if you prefer to eat your big meal in the middle of the day, feel free to indulge in one of these savory egg-centric dishes for lunch. A few jammy eggs on top of a salad transforms it from a side dish into a satisfying main meal, and the Toasty Holiday Strata (page 170) can help you use up all kinds of leftovers from the fridge, as well as lots of eggs.

SOUPS

Egg Drop Soup

Egg Lemon Soup (Avgolemono)

SALADS

Caesar Salad

Niçoise Salad

Warm Bacon and Eggs Salad

PASTA

Homemade Pasta

Pasta Carbonara

Ricotta Gnocchi

Browned Butter Sage Sauce

Baked Macaroni and Cheese

Egg Yolk Ravioli

MORE BAKED EGG DISHES

Toasty Holiday Strata

Bacon and Eggs Pizza

Baked Eggs in Butternut Squash Rings

Baked Eggs Marinara

Cheesy Mushroom Pie

Bacon and Beet Hash

Toad-in-the-Hole

EGG DROP SOUP

A staple of Chinese cuisine, egg drop soup more than any other type of soup highlights fresh eggs. This homemade version is so satisfying whenever I have the urge for a warm bowl of hearty soup. It's also easy to make—and ready before you can say "Chinese takeout." I usually use chicken stock in my soup, but to make this a meatless meal, substitute vegetable stock.

MAKES 4 TO 6 SERVINGS

8 cups (2 quarts) low-sodium chicken stock

One 2-inch piece fresh ginger, peeled and grated

1 teaspoon sesame oil, plus more for drizzling

1/4 cup cornstarch

1 teaspoon sugar

1/4 teaspoon ground turmeric

1/3 cup cold water

8 eggs, lightly whisked

4 scallions, sliced, plus more for garnish

Kosher salt

White pepper

In a medium-sized saucepan over high heat, stir the chicken stock, ginger, and sesame oil until it comes to a boil. Meanwhile whisk the cornstarch, sugar, and turmeric into the cold water in a measuring cup until smooth, then pour into the soup, whisking until combined. Reduce the heat to low and simmer the soup until thickened slightly, 1 to 2 minutes.

Using a wooden spoon, stir the soup in a circular motion while slowly pouring in the whisked eggs. Let the eggs cook for several seconds undisturbed, then remove the pan from the heat and gently stir in the scallions, being careful not to break up the egg ribbons. Season with salt and pepper, then pour the soup into bowls and garnish with scallions and a drizzle of sesame oil. Serve warm.

EGG LEMON SOUP (AVGOLEMONO)

The Greek word *avgolemono* translates to "egg and lemon" in English. This soup is quick and easy to make with simple ingredients you likely have on hand, like chicken stock and rice—and of course fresh eggs! Lemon juice and peel add a brightness to the soup, for a pick-me-up on a chilly evening. Plus, it's super-creamy without any heavy cream, so it's the ultimate comfort food without the guilt. And again, vegetable broth can be used in place of the chicken broth to make this a vegetarian option.

MAKES 4 TO 6 SERVINGS

8 cups (2 quarts) chicken broth

1/2 cup uncooked white rice

Kosher salt

Freshly ground black pepper

6 eggs

1/3 cup lemon juice (about 2 lemons)

Lemon slices for garnish

Fresh parsley for garnish

Grated lemon peel for garnish

In a large saucepan over medium-high heat, bring the broth and rice to a boil. Cover the pot, reduce the heat to low, and simmer until the rice is tender, about 12 to 14 minutes. Season with salt and pepper.

While the rice is cooking, in a medium-sized bowl whisk the eggs and lemon juice until light and frothy. Slowly whisk 1 cup of the hot broth into the whisked eggs, then whisk the egg mixture slowly back into the saucepan to keep the egg from curdling. Cook about 2 to 3 minutes, stirring continually, until the soup thickens and bubbles form around the edges. Be sure not to let the soup come to a boil, or the eggs may curdle.

Once the soup has thickened, remove it from the heat and season with more salt and pepper. Ladle the soup into bowls. Add a squeeze of lemon for added zing, then garnish with the parsley, lemon slices, and lemon peel.

CAESAR SALAD

Give me a bowl of crisp romaine lettuce drizzled with tangy, creamy homemade Caesar dressing and piled with garlicky baked croutons, and I'll happily eat the entire thing. This salad can go fridge to table in less than twenty minutes, making it an excellent option for a busy weeknight. Top it with some seared tuna, baked chicken, or grilled steak strips, and it turns into a hearty meal sure to please.

MAKES 2 GENEROUS DINNER SERVINGS OR 4 SIDE SALAD SERVINGS

Homemade Garlic Croutons

1 garlic clove, peeled and minced
1 tablespoon butter, melted
1 tablespoon extra-virgin olive oil
2 tablespoons freshly grated Parmesan cheese, plus more for garnish
1/4 teaspoon kosher salt
Freshly ground black pepper
2 cups bread cubes

For the Croutons

Preheat the oven to 350 degrees.

In a medium-sized bowl whisk the garlic, melted butter, olive oil, Parmesan, salt, and pepper until well combined, then add the bread cubes. Toss to coat all sides of the bread.

Spread the cubes in a single layer on a rimmed baking sheet. Bake until crisp and golden brown, about 12 to 15 minutes, flipping the cubes halfway through.

Caesar Dressing (page 258)

For the Dressing

While the croutons are baking, make the dressing as directed in the recipe.

Salad

1 head romaine lettuce

To Assemble the Salad

Chop the lettuce into chunks and place in a large mixing bowl. Toss with homemade garlic croutons and Caesar dressing, then divide between 2 salad bowls. Garnish with freshly shaved or grated Parmesan.

NIÇOISE SALAD

Niçoise salad calls for each ingredient to be tossed separately in the dressing and then arranged on the plate instead of mixed together. Traditional ingredients include those common in Nice, France, where the salad originated, including potatoes, green beans, fava beans, and tuna or anchovies. I've made some substitutions in this recipe, but the soft-cooked, jammy egg halves and Niçoise olives are a must!

MAKES 2 SERVINGS

Niçoise Dressing

1/2 cup extra-virgin olive oil
1 tablespoon stone-ground mustard
1/2 teaspoon mustard seeds
2 teaspoons honey
1/2 teaspoon champagne vinegar or white vinegar
Kosher salt
Freshly ground black pepper

For the Dressing

In a medium-sized bowl whisk the oil, mustard, mustard seeds, honey, and vinegar until blended. Season with salt and pepper.

Salad

2 cups lettuce or spinach
1/2 cup Niçoise olives
3 to 4 fingerling potatoes, parboiled and halved
1/2 cup snap peas, blanched
6 slices seared tuna
4 soft-cooked eggs (page 23)
1 tablespoon capers
4 sprigs fresh dill for garnish
4 sprigs fresh tarragon for garnish
Kosher salt
Freshly ground black pepper

To Assemble the Salad

To serve, divide the lettuce or spinach between 2 salad plates with the lettuce or spinach. Toss the olives, potatoes, and peas separately in the bowl of dressing, then arrange each ingredient in rows or piles on the plates. Add the tuna, then carefully cut the eggs in half and arrange them on the plates. Garnish the salads with the capers, dill, and tarragon, then season with salt and pepper.

WARM BACON AND EGGS SALAD

Bacon, eggs, toast, and orange juice—they're what breakfast is made of! Transform typical breakfast ingredients into a hearty dinner salad by adding mixed greens and a citrusy dressing. If you have some slightly stale bread on hand, this is the perfect way to use it. The stove-top croutons add a satisfying crunch to this dish.

MAKES 2 SERVINGS

4 slices Brown Sugar Maple Bacon (page 143)

Make the Brown Sugar Maple Bacon. While the bacon is baking, prepare the croutons, dressing, and eggs.

Homemade Buttered Croutons

3 tablespoons butter
2 cups cubed bread
1/2 teaspoon kosher salt

For the Croutons

Melt the butter in a medium-sized skillet over medium heat. Add the bread cubes, stir, sprinkle with salt, and let sit for a minute or two to brown on the bottom. Then cook for a few more minutes, stirring occasionally until the cubes are browned and crispy. Remove the croutons from the pan and drain on paper towels.

Orange-Ginger Dressing

1 teaspoon grated orange peel
1/3 cup freshly squeezed orange juice
1 tablespoon champagne vinegar
2 teaspoons extra-virgin olive oil
1/2 teaspoon freshly grated ginger
1/8 teaspoon kosher salt
Pinch of white pepper

For the Dressing

Combine the orange peel, orange juice, vinegar, oil, ginger, salt, and pepper in a half-pint Mason jar. Screw on the lid and shake until the dressing is well combined and smooth, about 20 seconds. Alternatively, whisk vigorously in a medium-sized bowl.

Salad

3 cups mixed salad greens

Butter for frying the eggs

4 eggs sunny-side up (page 29)

Half an orange, cut into pieces

Kosher salt

Freshly ground black pepper

For the Eggs

In the skillet add more butter and fry the eggs sunny-side up.

To Assemble the Salad

Remove the bacon from the oven. Divide the greens between 2 plates, then top each salad with 2 eggs, 2 slices of bacon, orange segments, and croutons. Drizzle with dressing, season with salt and pepper, and serve warm.

HOMEMADE PASTA

Homemade pasta is so much fun to make. Any type of flour, or combination of flours, will work: oo pasta flour, semolina, or all-purpose flour. The semolina is more rugged and will give the pasta more bite, while the oo flour is silkier. Don't have a pasta machine? No worries! You can knead the dough by hand, roll it out, then cut it with a knife to make fettuccine or tagliatelle.

MAKES ABOUT 1 POUND OF PASTA

1 1/2 cups OO pasta flour or all-purpose flour, plus more for dusting

1/2 cup durum semolina, plus more for dusting

1/2 teaspoon kosher salt

3 eggs, plus 1 egg yolk, lightly whisked

On a clean surface measure out the flour, semolina, and salt. Stir together with a fork. Then make a mound with an indentation in the center. Add the eggs and yolk to the center of the well and stir with a fork to combine, pulling in flour a little at a time from the sides of the well until the mixture is well combined.

Lightly flour your work surface and knead the dough about 10 minutes, until it forms a smooth ball. Use more flour, if necessary, to keep the dough from sticking, or add water if the dough is too dry. (Alternatively, use a stand mixer with a dough hook to knead the flour, semolina, salt, eggs, and yolk together on medium speed about 2 minutes, until smooth.)

Wrap the dough in plastic wrap and allow to rest for 30 minutes at room temperature (or overnight). After the dough has rested, cut it into 4 equal pieces. Wrap the dough in plastic wrap while you work with a piece at a time, to keep the dough from drying out. Roll each piece out with a rolling pin into a thin sheet or run it through a pasta machine to about a 1/16-inch thickness. Sprinkle the dough with flour if it gets too sticky.

Line a baking sheet with parchment paper and sprinkle it with semolina. Using the fettuccini attachment on your pasta machine, cut the sheets of dough into long strips. If you're cutting the fettuccine by hand, roll the pasta sheets up jelly-roll-style. Use a sharp knife to cut the rolls into 1/4-inch slices, making long, thin strips. (Or cut them into circles to make Egg Yolk Ravioli [page 167]).

Unroll the noodles and wind them into nests on the baking sheet while you cut the remaining noodles.

Let the noodles dry for at least 30 minutes. At this point you can refrigerate the noodles for up to 2 days or freeze them to cook later.

To cook, drop the noodles into a large pot of generously salted boiling water, stirring them to make sure they don't stick together. Cook the fresh pasta for about 2 minutes, until al dente. Refrigerated or frozen noodles will take a minute or two longer to cook.

PASTA CARBONARA

Carbonara is a simple, classic dish that uses a few basic ingredients to create a creamy pasta sauce. I often make it when we're low on food in the house, because who can't come up with pasta and some eggs? I also love this sauce because, unlike a rich, calorie-laden alfredo made with butter and heavy cream (which I'm a sucker for as well!), carbonara derives its creaminess from egg yolks and the pasta cooking water. A traditional carbonara recipe calls for cheese, but I typically leave it out, and the dish is still delicious. I like using tagliatelle for carbonara, but you can use spaghetti, linguine, or fettuccine.

MAKES 4 SERVINGS

4 to 6 quarts water

2 teaspoons kosher salt

2/3 cup finely grated fresh Parmesan or Pecorino Romano cheese, plus more for serving

4 egg yolks

Kosher salt

Freshly ground black pepper

1 pound fresh pasta

1 1/2 cups reserved pasta water

Fill a large pot with water and salt for the pasta and heat to a boil. In a medium-sized bowl whisk the cheese into the egg yolks. Season generously with salt and pepper.

When the water boils, add the pasta and cook until al dente, about 2 minutes for fresh pasta and a few minutes longer for dried. Just before the pasta is done, reserve 1 1/2 cups of the cooking water and then drain the pasta. (Tip: Setting a measuring cup next to your pasta pot before you boil the water will help you remember to reserve some of the cooking water. I can't tell you how many times I've remembered I was supposed to save some of the water as it's circling down the drain!)

Return the pasta to the pot after draining. Stir a little pasta water into the egg yolk mixture to loosen it up, then slowly stir the mixture into the pasta until well combined, adding more of the reserved pasta water a little at a time until the sauce is smooth and silky. Season with salt and pepper and serve with freshly grated cheese.

RICOTTA GNOCCHI

For years I never bothered to make my own gnocchi because the recipes that use potatoes seemed too labor intensive. But then I stumbled upon a recipe that substituted ricotta cheese for the potato and made it possible to have gnocchi on the table in less than thirty minutes. That was the beginning of my love affair with homemade gnocchi. May this recipe be the beginning of your love affair as well!

1 (15-ounce) container ricotta cheese

3 egg yolks

1 cup all-purpose flour, plus more for dusting

$1/2$ cup finely grated Parmesan, Asiago, or Pecorino Romano cheese

$1/2$ teaspoon ground nutmeg

$1 1/2$ teaspoons kosher salt, divided

Freshly ground black pepper

6 quarts water for cooking the gnocchi

2 tablespoons butter

Browned Butter Sage Sauce (page 165), extra-virgin olive oil, or Marinara Sauce (page 167) for serving

Place a paper towel in a colander in the sink and add the ricotta, then place another paper towel on top of the ricotta. Press down to soak up as much of the liquid as possible, then repeat with 2 fresh paper towels. Once the liquid has been absorbed, peel the paper towels off the ricotta and discard them.

In a large mixing bowl, whisk the drained ricotta with the egg yolks. Then add the flour, cheese, nutmeg, $1/2$ teaspoon salt, and pepper. Stir until combined. The dough should be semi-sticky and soft enough to be shaped into a ball. Overmixing the dough will make the gnocchi tough instead of soft and pillowy.

Flour a piece of parchment paper and a cutting board or clean work surface well—and rub flour on your hands. Be liberal with the flour as you form the gnocchi, adding more to the cutting board, the dough, and your hands when necessary.

Scrape the dough out of the bowl and pat or roll it into a flat, round disk on the floured work surface. Use a bench scraper to divide the dough into eight wedges. Roll each wedge into a rope, about 1 inch in diameter. Use a knife to trim off the ends, then cut the ropes at $3/4$- to 1-inch intervals to make individual gnocchi. Move the gnocchi to the parchment paper. Once you've cut all the gnocchi, sprinkle flour over the tops. (This helps prevent them from sticking together while they're cooking.)

Bring the water to a boil in a large pot over high heat. Add 1 teaspoon of salt. Carefully tip the gnocchi from the parchment paper into the boiling water, then stir them gently to keep them from clumping together.

Cook about 30 seconds, until the gnocchi float to the surface of the water, and then cook for 1 more minute. Use a slotted spoon to remove the gnocchi from the water, then drain them on paper towels.

Melt the butter in a large saucepan or skillet over medium-high heat. Once the butter has melted, add the drained gnocchi in a single layer. Separate the gnocchi into 2 batches to give them more room if needed.

To brown the bottoms, cook the gnocchi for 2 minutes without moving them. Then continue to cook for another couple of minutes, moving the gnocchi around in the pan gently until they're lightly browned all over. Don't be afraid to get a nice sear on some! Transfer the gnocchi to a bowl.

Serve with Browned Butter Sage Sauce, olive oil, or Marinara Sauce.

SAVING THE GNOCCHI FOR LATER

After the gnocchi are shaped, they can be frozen or stored in the refrigerator for later use. To freeze them, arrange them in a single layer on a baking sheet, freeze them until firm, then place them in a freezer bag or container. Cook them as directed in the recipe, dropping the frozen gnocchi into the boiling water in small batches. Alternatively, you can refrigerate the uncooked gnocchi, then cook them as directed. Uncooked gnocchi keep for up to 3 days in the refrigerator or up to 3 months in the freezer.

BROWNED BUTTER SAGE SAUCE

When my herb garden is bursting with fresh sage, I make this simple, yet remarkably decadent, sauce. Don't let the few basic ingredients deceive you: together, they create a rich, decadent sauce I love to toss with pasta or gnocchi or drizzle over fried eggs.

MAKES ABOUT 1/2 CUP

1/2 cup (1 stick) butter

5 to 6 fresh sage leaves

Kosher salt

White pepper

Chopped walnuts, optional

Melt the butter in a medium-sized saucepan over medium heat. Add the sage and continue to cook for several minutes, stirring occasionally, until the butter is foamy and begins to brown on the bottom of the pan, the sage is curled and crispy, and the sauce smells nutty and aromatic. Remove the sauce from the heat and season with salt and pepper. Sprinkle in some chopped walnuts if you desire.

BAKED MACARONI AND CHEESE

There are two basic recipes for baked macaroni and cheese. One uses a roux as the base, while the other uses eggs. Both are equally delicious. I mean, c'mon—you can't go wrong with macaroni, butter, cheese, and some seasonings—but when I have extra eggs, I always like to make this macaroni and cheese with its custardy egg-based cheese sauce.

Butter for greasing the
  casserole dish

8 cups water

1 1/2 cups milk, divided

1 1/2 teaspoons kosher salt,
  divided

8 ounces elbow macaroni

2 tablespoons butter, divided

1 cup shredded Cheddar cheese

1 cup shredded Gruyère cheese

1/2 cup heavy cream

1/2 cup reserved pasta cooking
  liquid

2 eggs

1/4 teaspoon grainy mustard

1/4 teaspoon white pepper

1/4 cup panko bread crumbs

Preheat the oven to 375 degrees. Use butter to grease an 8- or 9-inch square casserole dish.

In a large pot bring the water, 1 cup of milk, and 1 teaspoon of salt to a boil, then add the macaroni. Stirring occasionally, cook until the pasta is al dente, about 6 minutes. Reserve 1/2 cup of the pasta cooking liquid. (Tip: setting a measuring cup next to your pasta pot before you boil the water will help you remember to reserve some of the cooking water.) Drain the macaroni, then pour it into the prepared casserole dish.

Stir 1 tablespoon of butter into the macaroni until the butter melts. Sprinkle the cheeses over the macaroni. In a 2-cup measuring cup, whisk the cream, remaining 1/2 cup of milk, reserved pasta cooking liquid, eggs, mustard, remaining 1/2 teaspoon of salt, and pepper. Pour the mixture over the macaroni, making sure to cover it evenly.

Melt the remaining tablespoon of butter and stir in the bread crumbs. Sprinkle over the top of the casserole. Place the casserole in the oven and bake about 25 minutes, until the top is lightly browned and the cheese is hot and bubbly. Remove from the oven and allow to cool for 15 to 20 minutes before serving to allow the custard to set.

EGG YOLK RAVIOLI

These ravioli are deceptively simple to make using prepared wonton or egg-roll wrappers. However, if you're feeling ambitious, you can whip up your own pasta dough and roll out circles to encase the egg yolk filling. One ravioli on a bed of sauce makes a beautifully plated appetizer—or serve three or four ravioli per person as a main course.

MAKES 3 TO 4 DINNER SERVINGS, OR 12 APPETIZER SERVINGS

Marinara Sauce

7 to 8 medium tomatoes, cored and roughly chopped

1/2 medium onion, diced

2 garlic cloves, minced

5 to 6 fresh basil leaves, julienned

1 teaspoon kosher salt

1/8 teaspoon freshly ground black pepper

Ricotta Ravioli

3/4 cup ricotta cheese

1 tablespoon freshly grated Parmesan cheese, plus more for garnish

1 tablespoon shredded mozzarella cheese

Kosher salt for seasoning, plus 1 teaspoon for cooking ravioli

Freshly ground black pepper

Cornmeal for dusting

24 three-inch circles of dough (egg-roll, wonton, or homemade pasta sheets)

12 egg yolks

For the Marinara Sauce

In a saucepan over medium heat, cook the tomatoes, onion, and garlic until softened, 10 to 15 minutes, stirring occasionally. Break up any remaining large tomato chunks with a wooden spoon, then increase the heat and bring the sauce to a boil. Reduce the heat to low and simmer the sauce for another 15 to 20 minutes, stirring occasionally, until it thickens. Remove the pan from the heat and stir in the basil. Season with the salt and pepper. Makes about 2 cups.

For the Ravioli

In a small bowl stir the ricotta, Parmesan, and mozzarella cheeses together, mix well and season with salt and pepper. Dust a cutting board or clean work surface with cornmeal and lay out 12 of the dough circles. Spoon a tablespoon of the cheese mixture onto each of the dough circles and make an indentation in the center with the back of the spoon. Roll out the remaining dough circles to slightly enlarge them.

Set an egg yolk into each cheese indentation. Whisk the reserved egg white in a small bowl, then use a pastry brush to spread egg white along the outer edges of each circle. Top each egg yolk with one of the larger circles of dough, then firmly press the top and bottom dough edges together with your fingers to seal them. Be careful not to break the yolks.

When ready to serve, reheat the sauce. Bring the water

1 egg white

6 quarts water

Fresh basil, for garnish

to a gentle boil in a pot and add the teaspoon of salt, then carefully slide each ravioli into the water using a slotted spoon. Cook for 2 to 3 minutes or until the yolk is soft set. Ladle the sauce onto serving plates. Using the slotted spoon, remove one ravioli at a time from the water and place it on top of the marinara sauce. Garnish with the basil, Parmesan cheese, and salt and pepper.

PUMPKIN RAVIOLI

For a more elegant variation, try Pumpkin Ravioli. Whisk $1/2$ cup pumpkin puree, $3/4$ cup mascarpone, and $1/8$ teaspoon freshly grated nutmeg and substitute it for the ricotta and cheese filling. Then prepare the ravioli dough as directed. Serve the Pumpkin Ravioli atop a bed of Browned Butter Sage Sauce (page 165).

TOASTY HOLIDAY STRATA

The versatile strata is one of many recipes that helps you use up leftovers. You'll need bread, lots of eggs, milk, some cheese, and cooked meat, such as pork, ham, turkey, chicken, or ground beef. Don't eat meat? Then substitute some leftover cooked vegetables instead. Strata is also a wonderful holiday dish for entertaining because you can assemble it the night before—it's better if you let the bread soak overnight—then pop it into the oven the next day before your guests arrive. If desired, garnish your strata with fresh herbs from your garden.

MAKES 6 SERVINGS

Butter for greasing the pan

4 cups cubed bread

1/2 cup chopped cooked meat

1/2 cup minced shallots, scallions, or onions

2 garlic cloves, minced

2 cups shredded Swiss cheese (8 ounces), divided

8 eggs

2 cups milk

1/2 teaspoon ground nutmeg

Kosher salt

Black pepper

Minced chives, chopped green onions, or chopped fresh herbs (thyme, rosemary, basil, or sage) for garnish

Preheat the oven to 350 degrees. Use butter to grease an 8-inch square baking dish. Add the bread cubes and place the dish in the oven while it's preheating. Bake the bread cubes for 7 to 8 minutes until they're slightly toasted. Top with the meat, shallots, garlic, and 1 3/4 cups of the cheese.

In a medium-sized bowl whisk the eggs and milk and season generously with the nutmeg, salt, and pepper. Pour the eggs over the bread cubes and use a spoon or rubber spatula to fully submerge them in the liquid. Then let the dish rest for at least 30 minutes to make sure the bread soaks up lots of eggy liquid, or cover the dish in aluminum foil and refrigerate it overnight. If you refrigerate your strata, bring it to room temperature for about half an hour before baking.

Bake the strata for 20 minutes covered in aluminum foil, then sprinkle the reserved 1/4 cup cheese over the top and bake it uncovered for another 15 minutes, until the middle is set and the top is golden brown and crispy.

Remove the strata from the oven and let it cool slightly before cutting it into squares and garnishing with chives, green onion, or fresh herbs.

BACON AND EGGS PIZZA

Ever since college I've been a cold-leftover-pizza-for-breakfast kind of girl, but when there's no leftover pizza in the fridge, it's easy enough to quickly bake up this recipe. Borrowing the standard breakfast flavors of bacon, cheese, and eggs, my Bacon and Eggs Pizza gets an extra kick from fresh basil, scallions, and garlic. It has become our household's preference for pizza night. And the leftovers are delicious warmed up for breakfast!

MAKES ONE 12-INCH PIZZA

Extra-virgin olive oil, for brushing and drizzling

8 bacon slices, cut into 3/4-inch pieces

3 garlic cloves, thinly sliced

Freshly ground black pepper

Cornmeal for dusting

1 pound refrigerated pizza dough (or homemade)

15 slices pepperoni or cooked sliced sausage

8 ounces fresh mozzarella, cut into 8 slices

5 eggs

2 scallions, whites and greens thinly sliced

5 to 6 fresh basil leaves, chopped

Freshly grated Parmesan cheese for garnish

1/4 teaspoon crushed red pepper flakes

Hot sauce for drizzling, optional

Preheat the oven to 450 degrees. Brush a 12-inch pizza pan or rimmed baking sheet with olive oil.

In a large skillet over medium heat, cook the bacon and garlic until both are lightly browned but not crispy. Season the bacon and garlic with pepper and transfer to a paper-towel-lined plate to drain.

Dust a clean surface with cornmeal and roll out the pizza dough into a 12-inch circle. Press the dough into the pizza pan or for it on a baking sheet and brush with the tablespoon of olive oil. Top with the bacon mixture, pepperoni, and mozzarella.

Bake the crust in the oven for 10 to 12 minutes, until the edges start to brown. Remove from the oven, and without breaking the yolks, carefully crack the eggs onto the pizza, spacing them evenly.

Bake the pizza for another 8 to 10 minutes, until the egg whites are cooked, the yolks are partially runny, the cheese is melty and bubbling, and the outer edges of the pizza crust are browned.

Garnish the pizza with scallions and basil leaves. Grate some fresh Parmesan over the top, then sprinkle with red pepper flakes. Drizzle with olive oil and hot sauce, if desired.

BAKED EGGS

IN BUTTERNUT SQUASH RINGS

These baked eggs are such a fun way to use squash. I'm partial to butternut, but acorn or spaghetti squash would work equally well. Roasting the squash before adding the egg ensures that the squash will be tender and slightly caramelized, while the eggs will be cooked to perfection in the center.

MAKES 6 SERVINGS

1 large butternut squash

Extra-virgin olive oil

Kosher salt

Freshly ground black pepper

6 eggs

1/2 cup freshly grated Parmesan
   cheese

Fresh sage for garnish

Preheat the oven to 425 degrees. Line a rimmed baking sheet with parchment paper. Wash the squash and cut crosswise into six 3/4- to 1-inch slices. Scoop out the seeds and hollow out the middle of each slice to allow room for an egg.

Arrange the squash on the baking sheet and brush each ring with olive oil inside and out, then season with salt and pepper. Bake on the center rack of the oven for 20 minutes, until the squash has softened. Remove the baking sheet from the oven and gently crack and slide 1 egg into the center of each squash ring. Season with salt and pepper, drizzle with olive oil, and return to the oven. Bake about 8 minutes, until the egg whites are set and the yolks are firm but not fully set.

Use a spatula to slide the squash rings onto plates. Top with Parmesan, garnish with fresh sage, and drizzle with olive oil.

BAKED EGGS MARINARA

These marinara baked egg cups are wonderful served with garlic bread you can dip into the warm sauce and runny egg yolk. You can use your own marinara sauce recipe or try my quick marinara sauce recipe, which uses fresh summer produce from the garden.

MAKES 4 SERVINGS

Marinara Sauce

7 to 8 medium tomatoes, cored and roughly chopped

1/2 medium onion, diced

2 garlic cloves, minced

5 to 6 fresh basil leaves, julienned

1 teaspoon kosher salt

1/8 teaspoon freshly ground black pepper

Eggs

2 tablespoons extra-virgin olive oil, plus more for drizzling

1 clove garlic, minced

2 to 3 fresh thyme sprigs, plus more for garnish

Kosher salt

Freshly ground black pepper

4 eggs

1/2 cup grated Parmesan cheese

For the Marinara Sauce

In a saucepan over medium heat, cook the tomatoes, onion, and garlic until softened, 10 to 15 minutes, stirring occasionally. Break up any remaining large tomato chunks with a wooden spoon, then increase the heat and bring the sauce to a boil. Reduce the heat to low and simmer the sauce for another 15 to 20 minutes, stirring occasionally, until it thickens. Remove the pan from the heat and stir in the basil. Season with the salt and pepper. Makes about 2 cups.

For the Eggs

Preheat the oven to 400 degrees. Set four 4- to 6-ounce ramekins or cocottes on a rimmed baking sheet.

In a large skillet add 2 tablespoons of olive oil along with the garlic and thyme sprigs. Heat for 30 seconds on medium high, stirring until the garlic begins to brown and the thyme is aromatic. Add the marinara sauce, season with salt and pepper, and continue to cook for 3 minutes until slightly thickened and bubbly. Remove the skillet from the heat and discard the thyme.

Divide the sauce among the ramekins. Carefully crack an egg into each container, then top with the Parmesan and thyme. Drizzle with olive oil, then bake 15 to 16 minutes, until the egg whites are set (the yolks should still be runny) and the cheese is melted and bubbly.

Remove the baked eggs from the oven, drizzle with more olive oil, and garnish with fresh thyme. Season with salt and pepper.

CHEESY MUSHROOM PIE

For this hearty "pie," use any type of mushrooms and cheese, though I prefer Fontina, which doesn't overpower the thyme and mushrooms. The pie is meat-free, but it's definitely filling enough to eat for dinner, and you won't even miss the meat.

MAKES 6 TO 8 SERVINGS

2 cups all-purpose flour

1 tablespoon sugar

$1/4$ teaspoon kosher salt

$1/8$ teaspoon freshly ground black pepper

13 tablespoons (1 $1/2$ sticks plus 1 tablespoon) butter, cut into $1/2$-inch cubes and divided

2 eggs plus 1 yolk

Cornmeal for dusting, plus 2 tablespoons

5 cups thinly sliced mushrooms (about 12 ounces)

3 to 4 fresh thyme sprigs, plus more for garnish

3 cups shredded Fontina cheese (12 ounces)

$1/2$ cup freshly grated Parmesan cheese, divided

2 tablespoons cornmeal, divided

Extra-virgin olive oil

In a food processor, pulse the flour, sugar, salt, and pepper to combine. Add 12 tablespoons of cubed butter and pulse until the butter is incorporated and the mixture looks like wet sand. In a small bowl whisk the eggs plus the extra yolk, then add to the food processor in a slow stream while the motor is running. Process about 30 to 40 seconds, until the dough forms a ball.

Sprinkle a thin layer of cornmeal on a clean surface and, using a rolling pin, roll out the dough to an 11- to 12-inch circle. Press the dough into the bottom of a 9-inch springform pan and up the sides about an inch. Run a butter knife along the top edge of the dough, making a clean, even top. Refrigerate the crust for 30 minutes.

Preheat the oven to 400 degrees and place a rack in the center.

While the crust is chilling, melt the remaining tablespoon of butter in a large skillet over medium heat, then add the mushrooms and thyme. Cook 3 to 4 minutes, stirring occasionally, until the mushrooms are browned. Remove the skillet from the heat and discard the thyme.

Mix the Fontina and $1/4$ cup of the Parmesan cheese in a bowl.

Remove the chilled crust from the refrigerator and sprinkle with 1 tablespoon of cornmeal. Top with $1/3$ of the mushroom mixture and half of the cheese mixture. Repeat the layer, starting with the remaining 1 tablespoon of cornmeal, then half of the remaining mushrooms and all of the remaining cheese mixture. Arrange the last of the mushrooms on top, then sprinkle with the remaining $1/4$ cup Parmesan cheese. Drizzle the pie with olive oil.

Bake for 20 to 25 minutes, until the crust is golden brown and the cheese is melted and bubbly. Remove the pan from the oven, transfer to a wire rack, and let the pie cool for 10 to 15 minutes. Remove the sides of the springform pan. Drizzle the pie with more olive oil, slice into wedges, garnish with fresh thyme, and serve warm or at room temperature.

Store leftovers covered in the refrigerator and eat within 2 to 3 days.

REPURPOSE YOUR DOUGH

Whenever possible, I try not to let any ingredients or food go to waste. And leftover dough is no exception! If you have any dough remaining after you roll out your crust, you can save it to make my Butter Crackers (page 144). Roll the dough into a ball, wrap it in plastic wrap, and refrigerate it for two to three days or freeze it for up to one month.

BACON AND BEET HASH

I was never a big fan of hash until we moved to Maine. But I have to tell you, New Englanders really know how to make hash! Traditionally a mixture of meat, potatoes, onions, and spices often topped with an egg, hash was originally a way to use up leftovers from dinner and stretch meat further. "Red flannel" hash, made with beets instead of potatoes is extraordinary! This Bacon and Beet Hash is a satisfying cool-weather meal that I make often in the winter.

MAKES 4 TO 6 SERVINGS

4 beets, cut into 1/2-inch cubes

1 red onion, cut into 1-inch pieces

Extra-virgin olive oil

4 fresh rosemary sprigs, plus more for garnish

1 teaspoon ground cinnamon

Kosher salt

Freshly ground black pepper

8 slices bacon, cut into 1-inch pieces

1 pound ground beef

1 cup shredded Cheddar cheese (4 ounces)

8 eggs

1/2 cup sliced scallions

Preheat the oven to 450 degrees and place a rack in the upper third of the oven. Toss the beets and onion on a rimmed baking sheet with a drizzle of olive oil, then arrange them in a single layer. Lay the rosemary sprig on top, then sprinkle the mixture with cinnamon, salt, and pepper. Roast for 15 to 20 minutes in the oven or until the beets are soft enough to pierce with a fork. Remove the baking sheet from the oven and discard the rosemary.

While the vegetables are roasting, cook the bacon in a large oven-safe skillet over medium heat, moving the bacon around in the pan until it's crispy and browned, about 3 to 4 minutes. Drain the bacon on a paper-towel-lined plate. In the same skillet brown the beef, breaking it up as it cooks. Once no pink remains, remove the pan from the heat, drain any excess fat, and season the ground beef with salt and pepper.

Add the roasted vegetables and cooked bacon to the skillet with the ground beef and toss to combine. Sprinkle the top of the hash with Cheddar cheese. Using a spoon, make 8 divots in the mixture and carefully crack an egg into each, making sure not to break the yolk. Season the eggs with salt and pepper, then bake about 8 minutes, until the whites are set but the yolks are still runny.

Remove the skillet from the oven and spoon the hash onto plates, drizzling with olive oil and garnishing with sliced scallions and rosemary sprigs.

TOAD-IN-THE-HOLE

Imagine my surprise when I learned from a good friend that Yorkshire "pudding" isn't pudding at all but more like a big popover! Toad-in-the-Hole is basically Yorkshire pudding with sausages that supposedly look like toads poking their heads out of the ground. Despite its unappetizing name, it's delicious and easy to make.

MAKES 4 TO 6 SERVINGS

1 cup all-purpose flour

1 teaspoon kosher salt

Freshly ground black pepper

4 eggs

1 cup milk

2 tablespoons butter, melted

1 tablespoon stone-ground
   mustard, plus more for
   serving

Butter for greasing the
   casserole dish

12 ounces sweet pork sausage
   links (about 12 links)

Warmed maple syrup for
   serving

Preheat the oven to 400 degrees.

In a medium-sized bowl whisk the flour, salt, and pepper. In a second bowl whisk the eggs, milk, melted butter, and mustard until well combined and frothy. Slowly pour the egg mixture into the flour mixture and whisk until combined and smooth. Allow the batter to rest for 30 minutes.

Use butter to grease a 9-inch square casserole dish. Arrange the sausage links in the dish and bake in the oven until partially cooked, about 15 minutes, turning over halfway through.

Remove the casserole dish from the oven. Pour or spoon the batter into the dish and return it to the oven. Bake about 20 to 25 minutes, until the batter turns light golden, puffs up, and is crispy around the edges.

Remove the pudding from the oven, cut into wedges, and serve warm with more mustard on the side and a small pitcher of warmed maple syrup.

SWEETS

When you've gathered enough eggs for baking

We've finally arrived at my favorite chapter: desserts! I like to cook, but I *love* to bake. The organized, precise, numbers-oriented part of my brain gravitates toward the exact measuring and methods required for successful baking even more than the creative part of me loves the freedom and experimentation that's allowed in cooking.

Nearly every sweet treat contains eggs. (Scones and shortbread are exceptions and therefore are my best options when my chickens aren't laying and I want something sweet.) They work as a binder for the dry ingredients, provide flavor and color, emulsify liquids and fats, and act as a leavening agent to help baked goods rise.

I'm thrilled to share with you an array of desserts, from popular standards such as lemon meringue pie and Bundt pound cake to some personal specialties like my Pumpkin Swirl Cheesecake and Maple Walnut Cake. Years of living in New York, working in Manhattan, and dining in white-glove restaurants exposed me to fancy desserts like crème brûlée, meringues, and tiramisu—all of which are sure to impress dinner guests, but none of which are difficult to make. I hope you'll give them a try!

CAKES AND PIES

Angel Food Cake

Bundt Pound Cake

Cardamom Half-Pound Loaf Cake

Holiday Cranberry Half-Pound Loaf Cake

Cheesecake with Shortbread Crust

Pumpkin Swirl Cheesecake with Candied Walnuts

Boston Cream Pie

Lemon Meringue Pie

Maple Walnut Cake with Cream Cheese Frosting

Orange Brandy Olive Oil Cake

Rum Plum Breton

COOKIES AND MORE

Fancy Rolled Sugar Cookies

No-Roll Vanilla Cookies

Peanut Butter Cookies

Peanut Butter & Jelly Sandwich Cookies

Lemon Blueberry Whoopie Pies

Cream Puffs

Maple Chai Cream Puffs

Chocolate Cupcakes with Chocolate Swiss Meringue Buttercream Frosting

CLASSICS

Creamy Spiced Rice Pudding with Orange Sauce

Blueberry Cobbler

Crème Brûlée

Tiramisu

Lemon Curd

Vanilla Ice Cream

Mint White Chocolate Ice Cream

Roasted Rhubarb Clafoutis

Chocolate Pots de Crème

Blueberry Eton Mess

Mixed Berry Meringue Nests

ANGEL FOOD CAKE

Angel food cake is the first thing I remember baking with my mom. She showed me how to separate the eggs, then whip the whites and fold in the flour. As soon as the cake cooled enough to eat, we'd take turns tearing pieces off and shoving the light-as-a-feather cake into our mouths.

As long as your bowl and beater are clean, the whites should whip up well. And remember that eggs are easier to separate when cold from the fridge but whip up higher at room temperature. Before you start, grab your eggs from the fridge and separate them, then let the whites sit at room temperature for at least thirty minutes before you start beating them.

MAKES 12 SERVINGS

1 3/4 cups sugar, divided

1 cup all-purpose flour

1/4 teaspoon kosher salt

12 egg whites, room temperature

1 1/4 teaspoons cream of tartar

1 1/2 teaspoons vanilla bean paste

1/2 teaspoon orange extract

Topping Options

Confectioners' sugar for dusting

Fresh blueberries

Fresh mint

Preheat the oven to 325 degrees and place a rack in the bottom third of the oven.

In a medium-sized bowl whisk 1 cup of the sugar with the flour and salt. Use a stand mixer with a whisk attachment to beat the egg whites and cream of tartar on medium speed for 30 to 45 seconds until combined. Add the vanilla bean paste and orange extract. Increase the mixer speed to medium-high and beat until soft peaks form, about 2 to 3 minutes.

Slowly add the remaining 3/4 cup of sugar, while the mixer is running, until fully combined and stiff peaks form, about 2 minutes more. Remove the bowl from the mixer and sift in the flour mixture 1/4 cup a time, folding it gently into the batter with a wooden spoon or rubber spatula until it's incorporated and no flour clumps remain.

Spoon the batter into an ungreased 10-inch tube pan with a removable bottom, then run a long wooden skewer or knife through the batter to get the bubbles out. Finally, smooth the top with a rubber spatula.

Bake until the cake is golden brown, about 30 to 35 minutes, until golden brown on top and a toothpick inserted in the center comes out clean. Invert the pan on a wire rack or glass bottle to cool for at least 1 hour, then run a knife around the outer edge of the pan to release the sides of the cake.

Remove the cake and center insert from the pan, then run the knife around the center tube and along the bottom to unmold the cake. Place on a cake plate or stand and dust with confectioners' sugar. Cut the cake into slices with a serrated knife and garnish with fresh blueberries and mint or other preferred toppings. Store tightly wrapped with plastic wrap at room temperature for 2 to 3 days.

BUNDT POUND CAKE

I love the simplicity of a classic pound cake. And I'll let you in on a secret: it's one of the few things I can bake without a recipe! The standard recipe calls for one pound each of butter, sugar, eggs, and flour, with a pinch of salt and some vanilla bean paste if desired. This rich, dense cake needs nothing but a dusting of confectioners' sugar to serve as an elegant and satisfying dessert. It's also a way to use up a lot of eggs!

MAKES 12 SERVINGS

Butter and confectioners' sugar
     for the pan
3 1/2 cups all-purpose flour
1/4 teaspoon kosher salt
2 cups (4 sticks) butter, room
     temperature
2 cups sugar
8 eggs, room temperature
2 teaspoons vanilla bean paste
Confectioners' sugar for dusting

Preheat the oven to 350 degrees and place a rack in the center. Liberally grease a 10-inch Bundt pan with butter, then lightly dust with confectioners' sugar. Whisk the flour and salt in a small bowl.

Use a stand mixer with a paddle attachment to beat the butter and sugar on high speed about 5 minutes, until light lemon-yellow and fluffy. Add 1 egg at a time to the mixture and beat until incorporated before adding the next. Scrape down the sides of the bowl as needed. Add the vanilla bean paste and scrape down the sides of the bowl one last time.

Reduce the mixer speed to low and slowly add the flour mixture a little at a time until evenly combined. Spoon the thick batter into the prepared Bundt pan and smooth the top. Bake 55 to 60 minutes, until the top of the cake is golden brown and a toothpick inserted in the center comes out clean. Check after 30 minutes and if the cake is browning too quickly, tent a piece of aluminum foil over it.

Remove the cake from the oven and cool on a wire rack for 20 minutes, then run a butter knife along the edge of the pan to release the cake. Invert the cake to cool on the rack, then slice and serve, dusting the slices with confectioners' sugar.

CARDAMOM HALF-POUND LOAF CAKE

If I don't have enough eggs to make a full pound cake, I often make a half-pound cake instead. This cake bakes up in a regular loaf pan, and the cardamom and vanilla impart a nuanced flavor. To convert this recipe to a regular pound cake recipe, simply double the ingredients and bake in a Bundt or tube pan.

MAKES 1 LOAF

Half-Pound Loaf Cake

Butter and flour for prepping the pan
1 cup (2 sticks) butter, room temperature
1 cup sugar
4 eggs, room temperature
1 teaspoon vanilla bean paste
1 3/4 cups all-purpose flour, plus more for dusting
1 teaspoon ground cardamom
1/8 teaspoon kosher salt

Cardamom Glaze

1 cup confectioners' sugar
1 teaspoon ground cardamom
1 to 2 tablespoons milk

For the Cake

Preheat the oven to 350 degrees. Grease an 8 1/2 x 4 1/2-inch loaf pan with butter, then dust with flour.

Use a stand mixer with a paddle attachment to beat the butter and sugar on medium about 2 minutes, until light lemon-yellow and fluffy. Add 1 egg at a time to the mixture and beat until incorporated before adding the next. Scrape down the sides of the bowl as needed. Add the vanilla bean paste and scrape down the sides of the bowl one last time.

In a small bowl whisk the flour, cardamom, and salt. With the mixer set to low, gradually add the flour mixture to the batter and beat until blended. Use a rubber spatula to scrape the batter into your prepared pan and spread it evenly.

Bake about 55 to 60 minutes, until the cake is golden brown and a toothpick inserted in the center comes out clean. Cool the loaf in the pan on a wire rack for 15 minutes, then invert the pan and remove the loaf. Set the loaf on the rack to cool, about 1 hour, while you make the glaze, or overnight in the refrigerator.

For the Glaze

Whisk the confectioners' sugar and cardamom in a small bowl. Slowly add the milk and whisk until the sugar is incorporated and the glaze is smooth. Using a spoon or whisk, drizzle the glaze over the top and down the sides of the cake.

HOLIDAY CRANBERRY HALF-POUND LOAF CAKE

This festive half-pound loaf cake is one of my standard holiday recipes. It's quick and easy to make, and the presentation enhances any holiday dessert table. If you want to make a full pound cake, double the ingredients and bake in a Bundt or tube pan.

MAKES 1 LOAF

Cranberry Half-Pound Loaf Cake

Butter and flour for prepping the pan

1 cup cranberries, fresh or frozen

1 tablespoon plus 1 3/4 cups all-purpose flour, divided

1 cup (2 sticks) butter, room temperature

1 cup sugar

4 eggs, room temperature

1 teaspoon vanilla bean paste

1/8 teaspoon kosher salt

Topping Options

Handful of fresh cranberries

Sugared cranberries

Fresh rosemary sprigs

Confectioners' sugar

For the Cake

Preheat the oven to 350 degrees. Grease an 8 1/2 x 4 1/2- inch loaf pan with butter, then dust with flour. Toss the cranberries with the tablespoon of flour in a small bowl.

Use a stand mixer with a paddle attachment to beat the butter and sugar on medium about 2 minutes, until light lemon-yellow and fluffy. Add 1 egg at a time to the mixture and beat until incorporated before adding the next. Scrape down the sides of the bowl as needed. Add the vanilla bean paste and scrape down the sides of the bowl one last time.

Whisk the 1 3/4 cups of flour and the salt. With the mixer set to low, gradually add the flour mixture to the batter. Beat until blended, then use a wooden spoon or rubber spatula to fold in the cranberries. Use a rubber spatula to scrape the batter into your prepared pan and spread it evenly.

Bake 55 to 60 minutes, until the cake is golden brown and a toothpick inserted in the center of the loaf comes out clean. Cool the loaf in the pan on a wire rack for 15 minutes, then invert the pan and remove the loaf. Set the loaf on the rack to cool, about 1 hour, while you make the frosting and glaze, or up to overnight in the refrigerator.

Cream Cheese Frosting

¼ cup (½ stick) butter, room
    temperature
4 ounces cream cheese, room
    temperature
1 teaspoon vanilla bean paste
1 ½ cups confectioners' sugar

For the Frosting

Use a stand mixer with a paddle attachment to beat the butter, cream cheese, and vanilla bean paste on medium about 2 minutes, until smooth. Reduce the speed to low and slowly add the confectioners' sugar and beat about 2 minutes, until fluffy. Spread the frosting on the cooled loaf, then refrigerate for at least 30 minutes to set the frosting.

Sugared Cranberries

1 egg white
1 tablespoon of water
Fresh cranberries
Sugar

For the Sugared Cranberries

In a small bowl whisk 1 egg white with 1 tablespoon of water. Sprinkle a small plate with sugar. For as many sugared cranberries as desired, dip the cranberries in the egg wash, roll them in the sugar, and dry them on parchment paper.

White Chocolate Glaze

½ cup white chocolate chips
1 teaspoon coconut oil

For the Glaze

Melt the chocolate with the oil in a small saucepan over a double boiler, stirring until smooth. Add more oil if necessary until the glaze is a drizzling consistency. Slice the cake and arrange on individual plates, then use a pastry bag or spoon to drizzle the glaze over the slices. Garnish with either fresh or sugared cranberries and rosemary sprigs, and dust with confectioners' sugar, if desired.

CHEESECAKE

WITH SHORTBREAD CRUST

Everybody needs a basic cheesecake recipe in their repertoire, and this is mine. I'm not a fan of graham crackers, so I make a shortbread crust instead. In fact, this shortbread recipe is my most-used Christmas cookie recipe, since our chickens usual take their annual winter break around that time, and shortbread is one of the few cookie recipes that doesn't call for eggs. If you make shortbread regularly, investing in a decorative shortbread pan is fun, but a regular 8- or 9-inch square baking pan will work as well. For this cheesecake recipe you'll press the shortbread into a springform pan. For shortbread cookies, increase the baking time by 5 or 10 minutes, until they're lightly browned on top.

MAKES 12 SERVINGS

Shortbread Crust

Butter for greasing the pan
3/4 cup (1 1/2 sticks) butter, chilled
1/2 cup confectioners' sugar, plus more for dusting
1/4 teaspoon salt
1 1/2 teaspoons vanilla bean paste
1 1/2 cups all-purpose flour

For the Crust

Preheat the oven to 350 degrees and place a rack in the center. Bring a kettle filled with water to a boil. Use butter to grease the bottom of a 9-inch springform pan.

Use a stand mixer with a paddle attachment to beat the chilled butter on medium about 2 minutes, until it's light and fluffy. Beat in the confectioners' sugar, salt, and vanilla bean paste, scraping down the sides of the bowl as needed. Add the flour and continue to beat the mixture until the dough is combined and holds together when you pinch it. Dump the dough into the prepared pan and press across the bottom and about an inch up the sides. Use your fingers or the bottom of a drinking glass to press down on the dough, then prick it all over with the tines of a fork. Refrigerate the crust for 30 minutes.

After the crust has chilled, bake about 20 minutes until it's set. Remove the pan from the oven and let it cool slightly, then wrap the outside of the pan with 2 sheets of aluminum foil.

2 (8-ounce) packages cream
   cheese, room temperature

3 eggs, room temperature

1 cup sugar

16 ounces sour cream

Grated peel of 1 lemon (about
   1 tablespoon)

Juice of 1 lemon (about
   3 tablespoons)

2 teaspoons vanilla bean paste

1/8 teaspoon salt

For the Filling

Use a stand mixer with a paddle attachment to beat the cream cheese on medium 1 to 2 minutes, until smooth. Add 1 egg at a time to the mixture and beat until incorporated before adding the next. Scrape down the sides of the bowl as needed. Slowly add the sugar and beat on medium 2 to 3 minutes until smooth and creamy. Add the sour cream, lemon peel, lemon juice, vanilla bean paste, and salt and beat on medium for 1 to 2 minutes until just combined. Scrape down the sides of the bowl one last time.

Pour the filling into the cooled crust and spread evenly with a rubber spatula. Place the springform pan on a rimmed baking sheet and set in the oven on the middle rack. Pour the hot water from the kettle into the baking sheet so it comes partway up the sides of the sheet, about a 1/2 inch. Bake the cheesecake about 45 minutes, until the edges are set and the middle is still jiggly, then remove it from the water bath. It will firm up as it chills.

Cool the cheesecake in the pan on a wire rack for 1 hour, then cover the pan loosely with aluminum foil and refrigerate for at least 4 hours or overnight. To serve the cheesecake, run a knife around the outer edge to loosen it from the pan, then carefully unfasten the sides of the pan and transfer the cheesecake to a cake plate or stand.

PUMPKIN SWIRL CHEESECAKE

WITH CANDIED WALNUTS

Can't decide between classic cheesecake and a pumpkin pie this Thanksgiving? You don't need to when you make this elegant cross between the two. And the beauty of this quintessential dessert is that it can be baked the night before to make your holiday a little more stress free.

MAKES 12 SERVINGS

Gingersnap Crust

Butter for greasing the pan

4 tablespoons butter, melted

1 1/2 cups crushed gingersnap cookies (about 24 two-inch round cookies)

Pumpkin Swirl Cheesecake Filling

4 (8-ounce) packages cream cheese, room temperature

1 cup granulated sugar

3 tablespoons cornstarch

1 cup sour cream

2 teaspoons vanilla bean paste

3 eggs, room temperature

3/4 cup canned pumpkin puree

5 tablespoons firmly packed brown sugar, divided

1 tablespoon molasses

For the Crust

Preheat the oven to 325 degrees. Bring a kettle filled with water to a boil. Use butter to grease a 9-inch springform pan and wrap 2 layers of aluminum foil around the outside of the pan.

Pour the melted butter into a medium-sized bowl. Add the crushed gingersnaps, stir to coat the crumbs evenly, then press the mixture into the bottom of the pan. Refrigerate the crust until the filling is ready.

For the Filling

Use a stand mixer with a paddle attachment to beat the cream cheese, granulated sugar, and cornstarch on medium about 2 minutes, until smooth. Beat in the sour cream and vanilla bean paste, then add 1 egg at a time to the mixture and beat until incorporated before adding the next. Scrape down the sides of the bowl as needed. Pour half of the batter into a medium-sized bowl and set aside.

Into the remaining batter mix the pumpkin puree, 3 tablespoons of the brown sugar, molasses, cinnamon, ginger, cardamom, nutmeg, and cloves. Set aside 1 cup of the pumpkin batter.

Evenly spread half of the remaining pumpkin batter over the crust in the springform pan. Layer half of the plain batter

1 1/2 teaspoons ground
   cinnamon

3/4 teaspoon ground ginger

1/2 teaspoon ground cardamom

1/8 teaspoon ground nutmeg

1/8 teaspoon ground cloves

2 tablespoons butter

1 cup walnuts (whole or pieces)

Whipped cream, optional

on top of the pumpkin batter, then layer the remaining half of the pumpkin batter, followed by the remaining plain batter. Place dollops of the reserved cup of pumpkin batter on the top, then use a toothpick to swirl the batters to create a marbled design.

Place the pan on a rimmed baking sheet and set in the oven, then carefully fill the sheet partway, about 1/2-inch deep, with boiling water, making sure not to fill above the aluminum foil. Bake the cheesecake about 1 hour and 10 minutes, until the edges are set and the center of the cheesecake is still jiggly, then remove it from the water bath.

Cool the cheesecake in the pan on a wire rack for 1 hour, then cover the pan loosely with aluminum foil and refrigerate for at least 4 hours or overnight. To serve the cheesecake, run a knife around the outer edge to loosen it from the pan, then carefully unfasten the sides of the pan and transfer the cheesecake to a cake plate or stand.

To make the candied walnuts, melt 2 tablespoons of butter over medium heat in a skillet or frying pan. Add the walnuts and 2 remaining tablespoons of brown sugar and stir about 5 minutes. Continue to cook and stir the walnuts, until the sugar caramelizes and the walnuts start to smell nutty. Remove the nuts from the skillet and spread in a single layer on a piece of parchment paper to cool.

Garnish the cheesecake with the candied walnuts and dollops of whipped cream, if desired.

Note: You can also substitute 1 tablespoon of pumpkin pie spice for the cinnamon, ginger, cardamom, nutmeg, and cloves.

BOSTON CREAM PIE

With eggs in both the filling and the cake, this New England classic is a great way not only to use up some extra eggs but also to wow your dinner guests! While it does take time to pull together the three elements—the cake, the pastry cream filling, and the ganache topping— the end result is phenomenal. The pastry cream should be made first because it needs time to cool. And while it does so, you can bake the cake. Once both the cake and cream have cooled, it's a cinch to make the silky, chocolaty ganache to drizzle over the top.

MAKES 12 SERVINGS

Vanilla Pastry Cream

6 egg yolks, room temperature
1/2 cup sugar
2 tablespoons all-purpose flour
2 tablespoons cornstarch
1/8 teaspoon kosher salt
1 cup milk
1 cup heavy cream
2 teaspoons vanilla bean paste
1 tablespoon butter

Cake

Butter and flour for prepping
    the pans
2 cups all-purpose flour, plus
    more for dusting
2 teaspoons baking powder
1/4 teaspoon kosher salt
3/4 cup (1 1/2 sticks) butter, room
    temperature
1 cup sugar
3 eggs, room temperature
2 teaspoons vanilla bean paste
3/4 cup whole milk

For the Pastry Cream

In a medium-sized bowl whisk the egg yolks, sugar, flour, cornstarch, and salt until smooth.

Warm the milk and cream in a medium-sized, heavy saucepan over medium heat until the edges start to bubble. Remove from the heat. Slowly add the hot milk mixture, one ladleful at a time, into the egg mixture, whisking vigorously to temper the egg yolks so they don't curdle. Pour the egg mixture back into the saucepan and continue to cook over low heat, whisking constantly for 3 to 4 minutes until the mixture is bubbly and thick. Remove the pan from the heat and whisk in the vanilla bean paste and butter until the butter melts.

Transfer the pastry cream to a medium-sized bowl and press plastic wrap onto the surface to prevent a skin from forming on the top. Let the cream cool to room temperature, then refrigerate for at least 2 hours before using.

For the Cake

Preheat the oven to 350 degrees. Line the bottom of two 9-inch round cake pans with parchment paper, then grease the bottom and sides of the pans with butter and dust with flour.

In a medium-sized bowl whisk the flour, baking powder, and salt. Use a stand mixer with a paddle attachment to beat

the butter and sugar on medium speed about 2 minutes, until light and fluffy. Add 1 egg at a time to the mixture and beat until incorporated before adding the next, then add the vanilla bean paste. Scrape down the sides of the bowl as needed.

With the mixer set to low, alternately add the flour mixture and milk a little at a time. Mix until the batter is smooth, then divide it between the 2 pans.

Bake about 25 minutes, until the tops of the cake layers are light golden and a toothpick inserted into the center comes out clean. Cool the cakes on wire racks for 10 minutes, then loosen the sides with a butter knife and turn the cakes out onto a wire rack. Peel off the parchment paper and cool the cakes while you make the ganache glaze.

Ganache

2/3 cup heavy cream

6 ounces dark chocolate, chopped

For the Ganache

Heat the heavy cream in a small saucepan on medium, until bubbles start to appear around the edges. Add the chocolate to a 2-cup glass measuring cup. Pour the hot cream over the chocolate and let it stand for several minutes to melt the chocolate. Whisk the mixture until it's smooth, then let it sit while you assemble the cake to allow the ganache to firm up.

To Assemble the Cake

Invert one layer of cake onto a cake plate, with the bottom facing up. Add the pastry cream to a pastry bag with a 1/2-inch piping tip. Pipe the pastry cream around the outer edge of the cake first, then pipe dollops to cover the remaining cake surface. Top with the second layer of cake, then pour the ganache on top, letting some drip down the sides of the cake. Refrigerate at least 30 minutes to allow the ganache to set, then slice and serve.

LEMON MERINGUE PIE

Lemon meringue pie was my grandmother's favorite dessert, and every time I bake one, I think of her. I grew up across the street from my grandparents' chicken farm and spent many summer afternoons at their house. And I inherited my grandmother's love of lemons! Part of the beauty of this recipe is that you use both parts of the egg: the yolks are used in the filling, while the whites are used in the meringue topping.

MAKES 12 SERVINGS

Crust

1 1/3 cups all-purpose flour

2 tablespoons sugar

Grated peel of 1 lemon (about 1 tablespoon)

1/2 teaspoon kosher salt

1/2 cup butter (1 stick), chilled, cut into 1/2-inch cubes

4 to 5 tablespoons ice water

For the Crust

In a food processor combine the flour, sugar, lemon peel, and salt. Add the butter cubes and pulse several times, until the mixture looks like sand.

With the food processor running, pour in the ice water 1 tablespoon at a time, until the dough forms a ball. Remove the dough from the processor, flatten into a disc, encase in plastic wrap, and chill for at least 30 minutes.

Preheat the oven to 450 degrees. On a lightly floured surface, roll out the chilled dough into an 11- to 12-inch circle. Drape the dough over a 9-inch pie dish and trim the edges, leaving a 1/2-inch overhang. Fold the edge of the dough under itself, crimp, then prick the bottom of the crust with the tines of a fork. Chill the dough for 10 minutes.

Line the pie dough with 2 sheets of aluminum foil, weigh down with dried beans or pie weights, and bake in the oven for 10 minutes. Remove the weights and the aluminum foil and bake the crust for another 4 to 5 minutes until it is lightly browned. Remove the crust from the oven to cool. Reduce the oven temperature to 350 degrees.

Meringue

4 egg whites, room temperature

1 teaspoon vanilla bean paste

1/2 teaspoon cream of tartar

1/3 cup superfine sugar

For the Meringue

Use a stand mixer with a whisk attachment to beat the egg whites on medium speed 30 to 45 seconds, until frothy. Add the vanilla bean paste and cream of tartar, increase the mixer speed to medium-high and beat 2 to 3 minutes, until

soft peaks form. While the mixer is still running, slowly pour the sugar into the bowl. Beat the mixture on high speed another 2 to 3 minutes, until firm peaks form and the tips flop over slightly. To test the meringue's consistency, rub a little between your fingers. When the sugar has dissolved, the meringue will no longer feel gritty.

Lemon Filling

4 egg yolks

1 1/2 cups water

1 1/2 cups sugar

3 tablespoons all-purpose flour

3 tablespoons cornstarch

Pinch of kosher salt

3 tablespoons butter

2 teaspoons grated lemon peel

1/3 cup freshly squeezed lemon juice (about 2 medium lemons)

For the Filling

In a medium-sized bowl whisk the egg yolks.

In a medium-sized saucepan or pot, heat the water on medium-high. In a small bowl whisk the sugar, flour, cornstarch, and salt, then add the mixture to the water. Bring the water to a boil, whisking as the mixture heats. Once the liquid is bubbling, reduce the heat to low.

Ladle 1 cup of the liquid into the egg yolks and whisk to combine. Then slowly pour the egg mixture into the saucepan, whisking vigorously to keep the eggs from curdling. Turn up the heat and bring the liquid back to a boil, whisking constantly. Cook for 1 to 2 minutes until thickened.

Remove the pan from the heat and whisk in the butter and lemon peel, then slowly pour in the lemon juice. Whisk to combine.

To Assemble the Pie

Pour the warm filling into the pie shell. Using a rubber spatula, carefully spread the meringue over the top and right up to the piecrust to prevent the meringue from shrinking while it bakes. Use the spatula to make swoops and swirls in the meringue.

Bake the pie at 350 degrees, about 10 to 12 minutes, until the tips of the peaks are golden brown. Remove the pie from the oven and cool on a wire rack for 1 hour. Refrigerate the pie for at least 3 hours before serving to let the filling set so it will make a cleaner slice.

Store leftovers loosely covered in the refrigerator for a day or two.

MAPLE WALNUT CAKE

WITH CREAM CHEESE FROSTING

This dense, moist cake is packed with intense maple flavor and the heady crunch of walnuts, in both the batter and the rich, creamy frosting. It's the perfect sweet bite on a cold winter afternoon to accompany a mug of hot tea while watching the snow fall.

MAKES 12 TO 16 SERVINGS

Maple Walnut Cake

Butter for greasing the pan

2 1/2 cups all-purpose flour

2 1/4 teaspoons baking powder

1/4 teaspoon kosher salt

1 cup (2 sticks) butter, room temperature

1/4 cup firmly packed brown sugar

1 cup pure maple syrup, room temperature

1/2 cup sour cream

2 eggs, room temperature

1 teaspoon vanilla bean paste

1 cup chopped walnuts, divided

For the Cake

Preheat the oven to 350 degrees. Use butter to grease the bottom of an 8-inch square baking pan and line the bottom of the pan with parchment paper.

In a medium-sized bowl, whisk the flour, baking powder, and salt. Use a stand mixer with a paddle attachment to beat the butter on medium speed about 30 seconds, until light and fluffy. Add the brown sugar and beat another 1 to 2 minutes, until combined. Add the maple syrup and sour cream and beat to combine. Add 1 egg at a time and beat until incorporated before adding the next, then add the vanilla bean paste. Scrape down the sides of the bowl as needed.

With the mixer set to low, slowly add the flour mixture. Beat until combined, then stir in half of the walnuts.

Turn the batter into the prepared baking pan. Bake 40 to 45 minutes, until a toothpick inserted into the center comes out clean, the top of the cake is golden brown, and the center is set. Remove the cake from the oven and leave the temperature at 350 degrees.

Cool the cake in the pan on a wire rack for 15 minutes. Then remove the cake from the pan by running a knife around the edge and inverting the cake onto the wire rack. Remove the parchment paper and let the cake cool on the rack.

Spread the remaining walnuts on a cookie sheet lined with parchment paper and bake 10 to 12 minutes, until the nuts are lightly toasted and smell nutty.

Cream Cheese Frosting

4 ounces cream cheese, room temperature

1/4 cup (1/2 stick) butter, room temperature

Pinch of kosher salt

2 cups confectioners' sugar

2 tablespoons maple syrup, room temperature

For the Frosting

Use a stand mixer with a paddle attachment to beat the cream cheese and butter on medium about 2 minutes, until light and fluffy. Beat in the salt and confectioners' sugar a little at a time, then add the maple syrup and beat until smooth and creamy.

Once the cake has cooled, frost the top with the cream cheese frosting and sprinkle with the toasted walnuts. Cut into squares and serve.

ORANGE BRANDY OLIVE OIL CAKE

If you've never had olive oil cake, you're in for a treat! This recipe uses olive oil instead of butter, so keep it in mind if you're ever out of butter. Brush some boozy glaze on top, and you have a winner that will stay moist and deepen in flavor the longer it sits. I like to use Grand Marnier in the glaze, but it tastes delicious without the liqueur too.

MAKES 12 SERVINGS

Orange Brandy Olive Oil Cake

1 1/4 cups extra-virgin olive oil, plus more for prepping the pan

1 1/4 cups sugar, plus more for prepping the pan

2 cups all-purpose flour

1 teaspoon baking powder

1/2 teaspoon kosher salt

3 eggs, room temperature

1 cup milk

1/2 cup freshly squeezed orange juice

1/4 cup orange liqueur

1 1/4 cups sugar

Confectioners' sugar for dusting

For the Cake

Preheat the oven to 325 degrees. Brush the bottom and sides of a 9-inch round cake pan with olive oil, then cut a circle of parchment paper to cover the bottom. Set the parchment paper in place, brush it with more olive oil, then sprinkle with sugar.

In a medium-sized bowl whisk the flour, baking powder, and salt. Pour the olive oil into a large mixing bowl and add 1 egg at a time, whisking well to incorporate and emulsify the mixture. Whisk in the milk, orange juice, and orange liqueur.

Slowly pour in the sugar, whisking to incorporate, then whisk in the flour mixture until combined but not lumpy. Be careful not to overmix the batter. It will be thin, like pancake batter.

Pour the batter into the prepared pan. Bake 65 to 70 minutes, until the top of the cake is a dark golden brown. Remove the pan from the oven and cool it for 1 hour on a wire rack.

Orange Glaze

¹/4 cup orange juice

¹/2 cup confectioners' sugar

1 teaspoon orange liqueur,
   optional

For the Glaze

In a small bowl whisk the orange juice and confectioners' sugar until no lumps remain. Add the orange liqueur, if desired, and whisk to combine.

To Assemble the Cake

Run a butter knife around the outer rim of the cooled cake and invert the pan to remove the cake from the pan. Peel off the parchment paper and set the cake right side up on a wire rack. Brush the top with half of the glaze, then allow the cake to cool for another 1 to 2 hours, or cover to cool overnight in the refrigerator.

To serve, dust the cake generously with confectioners' sugar, slice it into wedges, and place the slices on plates, with the remaining glaze on the side for pouring. Store tightly wrapped at room temperature for up to a week.

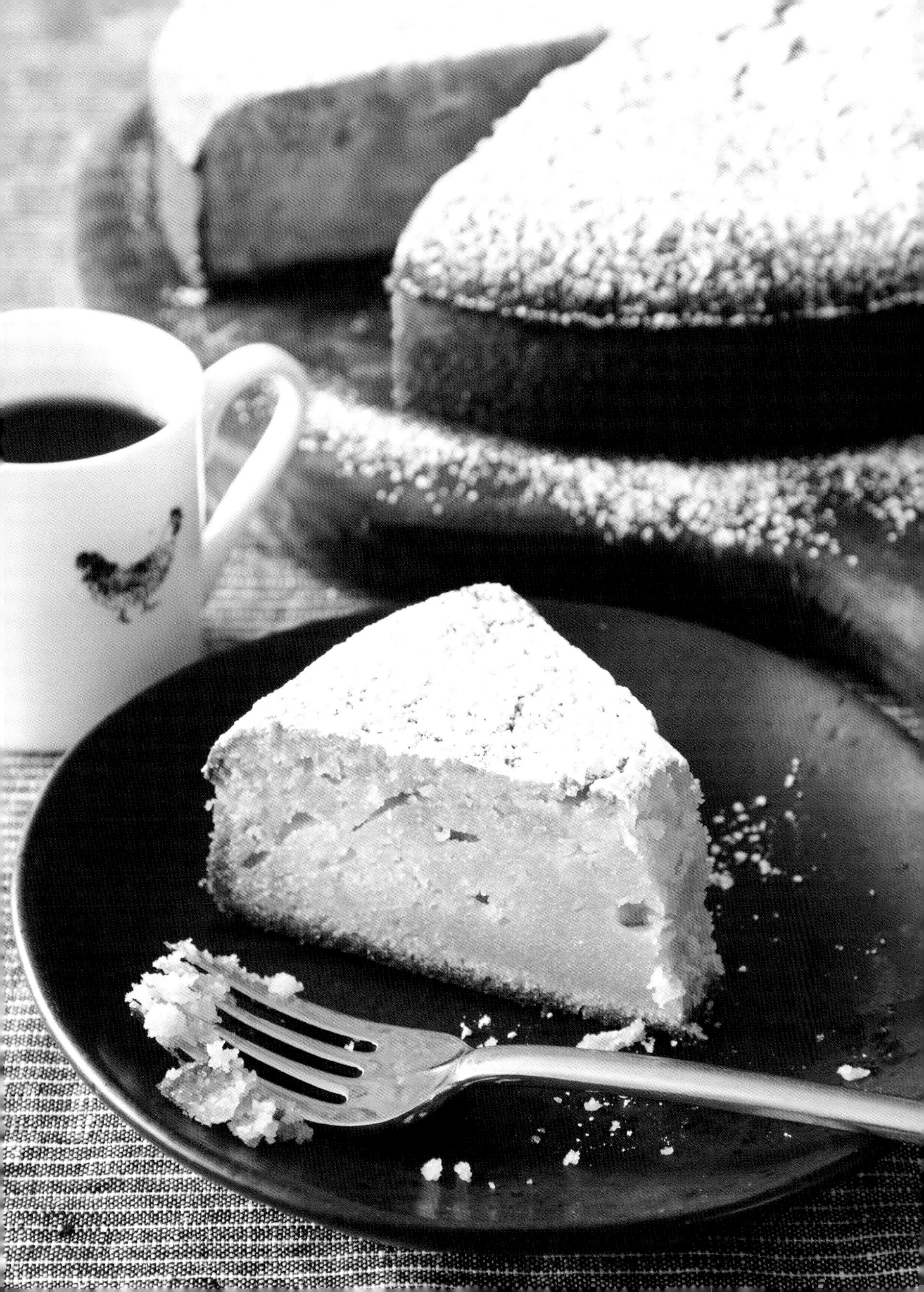

RUM PLUM BRETON

I once took cooking classes on Long Island at various local restaurants. Years later, I unearthed an old recipe card from one of those classes; the card was simply titled "Mango Breton." All I remembered about that dessert with the soft, buttery crust and juicy fruit filling was that it was one of the best desserts I'd ever eaten. I've swapped out the mangos for plums, but I left the rest of the original recipe mostly intact. I hope you enjoy it as much as I do. Though I hope the original pastry chef pardons my substitution, you have to admit that "Rum Plum Breton" has a certain je ne sais quoi.

MAKES 8 TO 10 SERVINGS

Butter for greasing the pan

1 cup (2 sticks) plus
    3 tablespoons butter, divided

1 cup plus 3 tablespoons sugar,
    divided

2 tablespoons dark rum, divided

4 egg yolks plus 1 whole egg,
    divided

2 3/4 cups plus 1 tablespoon
    all-purpose flour, divided, plus
    more for dusting

4 to 5 plums, pitted and thinly
    sliced (about 2 generous
    cups)

1 teaspoon lemon juice

1 teaspoon almond extract

Kosher salt

Preheat the oven to 350 degrees. Use butter to grease the bottom and sides of a 9-inch round cake pan and cut a piece of parchment paper to line the bottom of the pan.

Use a stand mixer with a paddle attachment to beat 1 cup of the butter on medium speed about 30 seconds, until soft. While the mixer is still running, slowly pour in 1 cup of the sugar. Beat about 2 minutes, until fluffy and combined. Scrape down the sides of the bowl, then add 1 tablespoon of the rum. Add 1 egg yolk at a time to the mixture and beat until incorporated before adding the next. Continue beating until the mixture is smooth, scraping the sides of the bowl as needed. Reduce the mixer speed to low and slowly add the 2 3/4 cups of flour until combined. The dough will be very soft. Let it rest while you make the filling.

Melt the remaining 3 tablespoons of butter in a large sauce-pan over medium heat. Add the plums, the remaining 3 tablespoons of sugar, the lemon juice, and the remaining tablespoon of rum. Stir to combine. Cook the liquid about 5 to 6 minutes, stirring occasionally, until the plums have softened but still hold their shape, and the liquid is thick and jammy. Remove the pan from the heat and stir in the almond extract.

Flour a piece of parchment paper or pastry cloth and roll out about 2/3 of the dough into a 10-inch circle. Invert the dough over the cake pan, then press into the bottom and

about an inch up the sides. The crust will be much thicker than a regular piecrust. Sprinkle with the remaining tablespoon of flour, then spread the filling over the dough. Roll out the remaining dough into a 9-inch circle, then place it on top of the filling. Trim as needed, then press down all around the edges to seal.

In a small bowl whisk the remaining whole egg with a pinch of salt and brush the top of the dough with the egg wash. Lightly score the top in a crisscross pattern with the tines of a fork. Bake about 50 minutes, until the crust is golden brown.

Cool the cake for several hours, or cool to room temperature and then chill overnight in the refrigerator. To serve, run a knife around the outer edge of the pan, then slice the cake into wedges and carefully lift them onto individual plates.

WHAT EXACTLY IS BRETON?

Breton is a type of dough that typically includes egg yolks and lots of butter. One reason it's popular with bakers is that it's so versatile. You can substitute different types of flour, such as nut-based, to create different textures and flavors, and the dough is easy to shape after it's mixed. Although my recipe uses the dough as a pie crust, you can also use it as a base for tarts, topped with a dollop of Lemon Curd (page 236) or fresh berries with some Crème Anglaise (page 264).

FANCY ROLLED SUGAR COOKIES

There's something deeply satisfying about rolling and cutting out cookies. This basic sugar cookie recipe is a holiday showstopper and a perfectly good everyday cookie as well.

MAKES ABOUT 36 COOKIES

Sugar Cookies

3 3/4 cups all-purpose flour, plus
  more for dusting
2 teaspoons baking powder
1/8 teaspoon kosher salt
1 cup (2 sticks) unsalted butter,
  room temperature
1 cup sugar
2 eggs, room temperature
1 teaspoon vanilla bean paste
1/4 cup heavy cream

Frosting

3 ounces cream cheese, room
  temperature
1 tablespoon milk
1 teaspoon vanilla bean paste
2 1/4 cups confectioners' sugar
Food coloring, if desired

For the Cookies

In a medium-sized bowl whisk the flour, baking powder, and salt. Use a stand mixer with a paddle attachment to beat the butter and sugar on medium speed about 2 minutes, until light and fluffy. Add 1 egg at a time to the mixture and beat until incorporated before adding the next, then add the vanilla bean paste. Reduce the mixer speed to low and alternate adding the flour mixture and heavy cream, mixing until combined into a soft dough. Scrape down the sides of the bowl as needed. Wrap the dough in plastic wrap and chill in the refrigerator for 2 hours or overnight.

Preheat the oven to 350 degrees and line 2 rimmed baking sheets with parchment paper.

Lightly flour a work surface and roll out the dough to about 1/4-inch thickness, then cut with a 3-inch round, scalloped cookie cutter. Place the cookies 1 inch apart on the baking sheets. Bake about 12 to 14 minutes, until the edges and bottoms are lightly brown. Cool the cookies on the baking sheets for 5 to 7 minutes, then move them to wire racks.

For the Frosting

Use a stand mixer with a paddle attachment to beat the cream cheese, milk, and vanilla bean paste on medium about 2 minutes, until smooth. Gradually add the confectioners' sugar, beating until combined. If desired, divide the frosting into individual bowls, add a few drops of food coloring to each bowl, and stir to incorporate.

Once the cookies cool, frost them using a pastry bag with a basket-weave piping tip.

NO-ROLL VANILLA COOKIES

I love to whip up these cookies on a whim. The cookie dough is superfast to make because it doesn't require any chilling or rolling out. These cookies are bursting with vanilla flavor and are thick, soft, and chewy inside. You can eat them plain or frost them with any type of frosting you like, but they'll be extra festive topped with my Swiss Meringue Buttercream Frosting (page 276) and some Homemade Sprinkles (page 278).

MAKES ABOUT 40 COOKIES

5 1/2 cups all-purpose flour

1/2 teaspoon baking soda

1/2 teaspoon cream of tartar

1 teaspoon kosher salt

2 sticks (1 cup) butter, room temperature

1 1/4 cups granulated sugar

3/4 cup confectioners' sugar

3/4 cup vegetable oil

2 eggs

2 tablespoons milk

1 tablespoon vanilla bean paste

Preheat the oven to 350 degrees. Line 2 rimmed baking sheets with parchment paper.

In a medium-sized bowl whisk the flour, baking soda, cream of tartar, and salt.

Use a stand mixer with a paddle attachment to beat the butter on medium speed about 2 minutes, until smooth. Reduce the mixer speed to low and beat in the granulated sugar and the confectioners' sugar. While the mixer is still running, add the oil and then the eggs 1 at a time, beating until incorporated before adding the next. Then add the milk and vanilla bean paste. Increase the mixer speed to medium and combine until smooth, scraping the bowl as needed. Decrease the mixer speed to low and slowly add the flour mixture, mixing until the flour is incorporated.

Using a #30 disher-style ice cream scoop or spoon, scoop out golf-ball-size balls of dough, about 2 tablespoons apiece onto ungreased rimmed baking sheets, spacing them 2 inches apart. Flatten the balls with the bottom of a glass to about 1/2-inch thickness. Bake each batch about 10 to 12 minutes, until the bottoms of the cookies are slightly browned. Cool the cookies on the baking sheets for 5 to 7 minutes, then move them to wire racks to cool.

Swirl some Swiss Meringue Buttercream Frosting onto the cooled cookies with an offset spatula, then decorate them with Homemade Sprinkles.

PEANUT BUTTER COOKIES

My husband was in the navy during the early years of our marriage. He mostly worked on ships, but his last few tours were in a submarine. He came home from one deployment with a recipe and a bag of clothes stinking of diesel fuel. That was out of the ordinary, to say the least (the recipe, not the fuel smell!). He told me that the peanut butter cookies they'd been served at sea were the best he'd ever eaten. He somehow cajoled the cook into giving him the recipe, which I've made many times over the years, with a few modifications. I replaced the shortening with butter and the vanilla extract with vanilla bean paste. I also reduced the yield to a manageable number. The original recipe made about nine dozen cookies!

MAKES ABOUT 30 COOKIES

2 cups all-purpose flour

1/2 teaspoon baking soda

1/4 teaspoon kosher salt

11 tablespoons butter, room temperature

1 cup plus 1 tablespoon granulated sugar, divided

1/2 cup firmly packed light brown sugar

2 eggs

1 teaspoon vanilla bean paste

1 cup creamy or chunky peanut butter

Preheat the oven to 325 degrees. In a small bowl whisk the flour, baking soda, and salt.

Use a stand mixer with a paddle attachment to beat the butter, 1 cup of granulated sugar, and the brown sugar on medium speed about 2 minutes, until light and fluffy. Add 1 egg at a time to the mixture and beat until incorporated before adding the next. Scrape down the sides of the bowl as needed. Add the vanilla bean paste and peanut butter and mix until smooth. Scrape down the sides of the bowl one last time. Reduce the mixer speed to low and slowly add the flour mixture, beating until combined.

Using a #30 disher-style ice cream scoop or spoon, scoop out balls of dough about 2 tablespoons apiece onto ungreased rimmed baking sheets, spacing them 2 inches apart. Pour the remaining tablespoon of granulated sugar onto a small plate and press the tines of a fork into it. Use the fork to make a crisscross pattern on the top of each ball, flattening each to about 1/2-inch thickness, pressing the tines back into the sugar as necessary.

Bake about 16 to 18 minutes until the cookies are lightly browned around the edges. Cool for 5 minutes on the baking sheets, then move the cookies to a wire rack to cool, about 30 minutes.

PEANUT BUTTER & JELLY SANDWICH COOKIES

Peanut butter cookies are a fitting vehicle for cookie sandwiches. I love using a berry cream cheese filling that turns them into peanut butter and jelly sandwich cookies. And why not add a dollop of marshmallow crème as well, for a trip back to childhood and those fluffernutter sandwiches?

MAKES 15 SANDWICH COOKIES

30 Peanut Butter Cookies
(page 216)

Jelly Filling

4 ounces cream cheese, room
temperature

4 tablespoons butter, room
temperature

1/2 teaspoon vanilla bean paste

2 tablespoons blackberry jam or
other flavor jam or jelly

1/8 teaspoon kosher salt

1 1/2 cups confectioners' sugar,
plus more for dusting

Marshmallow Crème topping,
optional (page 274)

Use a stand mixer with a paddle attachment to beat the cream cheese, butter, vanilla bean paste, jam, and salt on medium-low about 2 minutes, until smooth. Gradually add the confectioners' sugar, beating until incorporated and the filling is light and fluffy.

Spread half the cooled Peanut Butter Cookies with the filling, allowing about 1 tablespoon per cookie, add some marshmallow crème if desired, then top with the remaining cookies.

LEMON BLUEBERRY WHOOPIE PIES

I'd never eaten a whoopie pie until we moved to Maine. Although the origin of the whoopie pie is disputed, it turns out that the birthplace is right here in Lewiston, Maine. The whoopie pie is Maine's official treat, and blueberry pie is the official state dessert. Whoopie pies come in various of flavors, but I've combined two Maine staples in my Lemon Blueberry Whoopie Pie recipe. The recipe calls for buttermilk, but curdling regular milk with lemon juice works fine if you don't have buttermilk.

MAKES 12 WHOOPIE PIES

Blueberry Jam

1/2 cup blueberries

1/2 cup sugar

Grated peel of 1 lemon (about
    1 tablespoon)

Whoopie Pies

2 1/2 cups all-purpose flour

2 teaspoons baking powder

1/4 teaspoon kosher salt

1/2 cup (1 stick) butter, room
    temperature

1 cup sugar

2 eggs

1 teaspoon vanilla bean paste

Grated peel of 1 lemon (about
    1 tablespoon)

2/3 cup buttermilk (or
    2 teaspoons lemon juice plus
    milk to equal 2/3 cup)

For the Whoopie Pies

Preheat the oven to 350 degrees. Line 2 rimmed baking sheets with parchment paper.

In a small bowl whisk the flour, baking powder, and salt.

Use a stand mixer with a paddle attachment to beat the butter and sugar on medium speed about 2 minutes, until light and fluffy. Add 1 egg at a time to the mixture and beat until incorporated before adding the next. Then add the vanilla bean paste and lemon peel and beat until combined. Reduce the mixer speed to low and alternate adding the flour mixture and buttermilk. Beat until smooth and combined. Scrape down the sides of the bowl as needed.

Using a 1 3/4-inch cookie scoop, drop the dough, about 2 tablespoons each, onto the baking sheets, spacing the mounds 2 inches apart. You should have 24 mounds. Bake 10 to 12 minutes, until the cookies are a light golden brown and the tops are springy when pressed. Cool the cookies for 5 minutes on the baking sheets, then move to wire racks to cool at least 30 minutes, while you prepare the filling.

4 ounces cream cheese, room
 temperature
4 tablespoons butter, room
 temperature
1 $\frac{1}{4}$ cups confectioners' sugar
$\frac{1}{4}$ cup blueberry jam

For the Jam

In a small saucepan, cook the
blueberries, sugar, and lemon
peel over medium heat 3 to 4
minutes, until thick and bubbly.
Set aside to cool.

For the Filling

Use a stand mixer with a whisk attachment to beat the
cream cheese and butter on medium about 2 minutes, until
creamy. Add the confectioners' sugar and beat until smooth
and combined. Stir in the blueberry jam.

Spread the filling onto half of the cooled pies and top with
the remaining pies.

CREAM PUFFS

Cream puffs require making a pâte à choux dough, an egg-based dough that's started on the stove and finished with a mixer. Once you master the basic cream puff recipe, you'll find yourself filling these airy puffs not only with sweet fillings like whipped cream or pastry cream but also with savory chicken, tuna, or egg salad.

MAKES 15 TO 16 CREAM PUFFS

Choux Pastry

1 cup water

1/2 cup (1 stick) butter, cut into pats

1 tablespoon sugar

1/4 teaspoon salt

1 cup all-purpose flour

4 eggs

Confectioners' sugar for dusting, optional

For the Choux

Preheat the oven to 425 degrees and line a rimmed baking sheet with parchment paper.

In a large, heavy saucepan, combine the water, butter, sugar, and salt and cook over low heat, stirring occasionally with a wooden spoon until the butter melts and bubbles start to form around the edges of the pan. Pour in all the flour and stir vigorously for 2 to 3 minutes, until the mixture forms a ball and pulls away from the sides of the pan, leaving a film. Remove the pan from the heat.

To slightly cool the dough, use a stand mixer with a paddle attachment to beat the ball of dough on medium-high speed about 1 to 2 minutes. Add 1 egg at a time to the mixture and beat until incorporated before adding the next. Continue beating until the dough is smooth and glossy.

Drop the dough by 1/4 cupfuls onto the baking sheet, or use a pastry bag and pipe the dough, into 2-inch mounds spaced 2 to 3 inches apart.

Bake the pastry about 20 minutes without opening the oven, until golden brown. Then turn off the oven, prick the side of each puffed pastry with a toothpick to release the steam, and leave the puffs in the oven with the door propped open for another 10 minutes.

Remove the puffs from the oven and allow them to cool while you make the filling.

Whipped Cream Filling

1 cup heavy cream

3 tablespoons sugar

1 teaspoon vanilla bean paste

Pinch of salt

For the Filling

Use a stand mixer with a whisk attachment to beat the cream, sugar, vanilla bean paste, and salt on medium-high about 5 minutes, until stiff peaks form.

When the puffs are cool, split them in half and fill them with a dollop of the whipped cream. Dust with confectioners' sugar, if desired.

MAPLE CHAI CREAM PUFFS

A variation on a classic cream puff recipe, these Maple Chai Cream Puffs are a delicacy. I put maple syrup and chai spice in the cream cheese filling and replace the sugar in the choux dough with maple syrup for a warm winter flavor.

MAKES 15 TO 16 CREAM PUFFS

Choux Pastry

1 cup water

1/2 cup (1 stick) butter, cut into pats

1 tablespoon maple syrup

1/4 teaspoon kosher salt

1 cup all-purpose flour

4 eggs, room temperature

Confectioners' sugar for dusting, optional

Maple syrup for drizzling, optional

Maple Chai Cream Cheese Filling

2 (8-ounce) packages cream cheese, room temperature

1 cup confectioners' sugar

2 teaspoons chai spice powder

3 tablespoons maple syrup

For the Choux

Preheat the oven to 425 degrees and line a rimmed baking sheet with parchment paper.

In a large, heavy saucepan, combine the water, butter, maple syrup, and salt and cook over low heat, stirring occasionally with a wooden spoon until the butter melts and bubbles start to form around the edges of the pan. Pour in all the flour and stir vigorously for 2 to 3 minutes, until the mixture forms a ball and pulls away from the sides of the pan, leaving a film. Remove the pan from the heat.

To slightly cool the dough, use a stand mixer with a paddle attachment to beat the ball of dough on medium-high speed about 1 to 2 minutes. Add 1 egg at a time to the mixture and beat until incorporated before adding the next. Continue beating until the dough is smooth and glossy.

Drop the dough by 1/4 cupfuls onto the baking sheet, or use a pastry bag and pipe the dough, into 2-inch mounds spaced 2 to 3 inches apart.

Bake the pastry about 20 minutes without opening the oven, until golden brown. Then turn off the oven, prick the side of each puffed pastry with a toothpick to release the steam, and leave the puffs in the oven with the door propped open for another 10 minutes.

Remove the puffs from the oven and allow them to cool while you make the filling.

For the Filling

Use a stand mixer with a whisk attachment to beat the cream cheese, confectioners' sugar, chai spice, and maple syrup on medium about 2 minutes, until well combined, light, and fluffy.

When the puffs are cool, split them in half and fill them with a dollop of the filling. Dust with confectioners' sugar and drizzle with maple syrup, if desired.

CHOCOLATE CUPCAKES

WITH CHOCOLATE SWISS MERINGUE BUTTERCREAM FROSTING

Everyone needs a decadent chocolate cupcake recipe in their repertoire, and this one will knock your socks off! Splurge on the best cocoa you can find. Instead of using coffee crystals like other recipes, I brew a pot of coffee and measure out a $1/2$ cup for this recipe. Instead of buttermilk, regular milk mixed with white vinegar will give this recipe the acid it needs, and the mascarpone cheese imparts moisture. Walnut oil to adds a hint of nutty flavor, but any vegetable oil works.

MAKES 18 CUPCAKES

Chocolate Cupcakes

1/2 cup milk

1/2 teaspoon white vinegar

1 1/4 cups all-purpose flour

2/3 cup unsweetened cocoa

1 1/2 teaspoons baking powder

1/2 teaspoon baking soda

1/2 teaspoon kosher salt

3/4 cup granulated sugar

1/2 cup firmly packed dark
   brown sugar

1 egg, plus 1 egg yolk

1/4 cup mascarpone cheese

1/4 cup walnut oil

2 teaspoons vanilla bean paste

1/2 cup strong brewed coffee,
   room temperature

Chocolate Swiss Meringue
Buttercream Frosting
(page 276)

Homemade Sprinkles for
   garnish (page 278)

For the Cupcakes

Preheat the oven to 350 degrees and line 18 cupcake cups with paper liners. Pour the milk into a measuring cup and add the vinegar.

In a large bowl whisk the flour, cocoa, baking powder, baking soda, and salt. Add the granulated sugar and brown sugar and stir until no lumps remain. In a medium-sized bowl whisk the egg, egg yolk, mascarpone, oil, and vanilla bean paste. Whisk the egg mixture into the flour mixture. Slowly add the coffee and whisk until the batter is glossy and smooth. The batter will be thinner than a standard cake batter.

Using a ladle, fill each baking cup with batter a little more than halfway, then divide any remaining batter evenly among the cups. Bake the cupcakes about 14 to 15 minutes, until a toothpick inserted in the center comes out clean. Cool the cupcakes in the pan for a few minutes, then move them to a wire rack to cool.

For the Frosting

Make the frosting as directed in the recipe.

Using an offset spatula, spread the frosting onto the cooled cupcakes, then garnish with sprinkles.

CREAMY SPICED RICE PUDDING

WITH ORANGE SAUCE

Finnish rice pudding is typically flavored with vanilla and cinnamon and has a berry topping, but I love to add warming holiday spices and a sweet orange sauce instead of berries. Preparing this dish low and slow is the key to the creamy texture, so don't rush.

MAKES 4 SERVINGS

Spiced Rice Pudding

3 cups milk

1/2 cup white rice

1 teaspoon spices of choice
   (such as cardamom,
   cinnamon, ginger, nutmeg)

1/2 cup heavy cream, plus more
   for serving

2 egg yolks

1 teaspoon vanilla bean paste

1/4 cup sugar

1/4 teaspoon kosher salt

Orange Sauce

4 thin orange slices, plus 4
   slices for serving

Juice of 1 orange (about 1/3 cup)

1 tablespoon firmly packed
   brown sugar, plus more for
   serving

1 tablespoon butter

For the Rice Pudding

In a medium-sized saucepan, bring the milk, rice, and spices to a simmer over low heat. Cover and continue simmering about 20 to 25 minutes, stirring occasionally, until the rice is tender and the liquid has been absorbed.

In a medium-sized bowl, whisk the cream, egg yolks, vanilla bean paste, granulated sugar, and salt.

Once the rice is cooked, temper the egg mixture by adding a few spoonfuls of rice at a time to the egg mixture and whisking to combine. This will keep the eggs from cooking too fast and curdling. Add several more spoonfuls, then pour the egg mixture into the pot with the rice and cook over low heat 2 to 3 minutes, stirring to combine, until slightly thickened.

Remove the pudding from the heat and pour or spoon it into small dessert bowls. Allow it to cool slightly before serving or cover and refrigerate to serve later.

For the Sauce

Bring the orange slices, orange juice, and brown sugar to a boil in a saucepan over medium heat, stirring to dissolve the sugar. Cook about 2 to 3 minutes, until the sauce reduces slightly. Stir in the butter until it melts, then remove the sauce from the heat.

To serve the rice pudding, pour some heavy cream around the edges of each bowl, drizzle the top of the pudding with orange sauce, garnish with an orange slice, and sprinkle with brown sugar.

BLUEBERRY COBBLER

Wild Maine blueberries make the best blueberry pies and cobblers, but if you can't find them, regular blueberries will do. I love a good blueberry pie, but when I'm short on time, this cobbler is the next best thing because it's quick and easy to assemble. Topped with a scoop of homemade Vanilla Ice Cream, it's my choice summer dessert when blueberries are in season, though I always make sure to store some bags of berries in the freezer so we can enjoy this dessert year-round.

MAKES 6 TO 8 SERVINGS

4 cups fresh or frozen
blueberries

1/4 cup firmly packed light brown
sugar

1 tablespoon cornstarch

Grated peel of 1 lime (about
2 teaspoons)

Juice of 1 lime (about
2 tablespoons)

1/4 teaspoon ground cardamom

1/4 teaspoon freshly ground
nutmeg

1 cup all-purpose flour

1/2 cup granulated sugar

1/2 teaspoon baking powder

1/8 teaspoon kosher salt

1 egg

1/4 cup milk

1/2 teaspoon vanilla bean paste

Vanilla Ice Cream for serving,
optional (page 237)

Preheat the oven to 375 degrees.

In an 8-inch square baking dish, mix the blueberries, brown sugar, cornstarch, lime peel, lime juice, cardamom, and nutmeg.

Whisk the flour, granulated sugar, baking powder, and salt in a small bowl. In a medium-sized mixing bowl whisk the egg, milk, and vanilla bean paste. Gradually add the flour mixture to the egg mixture and whisk until the ingredients are incorporated. Drop the batter by rounded spoonfuls evenly over the blueberry mixture, making sure to cover most of the berries.

Bake about 35 to 40 minutes, until the topping is golden brown and the filling is thick and bubbly. Remove the cobbler from the oven and let it cool slightly, then spoon it into individual bowls and top with ice cream, if desired.

CRÈME BRÛLÉE

I don't recall the first time I had crème brûlée, but one bite was all it took to fall in love. When I started raising chickens, I decided to try creating my own recipe, which was more delightful than any version I'd ever eaten. But it wasn't quite right. So I made it at least one hundred more times to perfect it.

Similar to other recipes with only a few ingredients, each ingredient in this recipe must be top-notch. Crème brûlée is all about the fresh eggs and the technique. Superfine sugar will brûlée the best, but if you don't have any, a coffee grinder or food processor can be used to grind regular sugar into smaller granules that will torch better.

This dessert has many variations that incorporate more ingredients, flavors, and toppings, but I don't want anything distracting me from that satisfying crack of the sugary shell and the smooth, decadent custard underneath.

MAKES 6

8 egg yolks

3 cups heavy cream

1/2 cup granulated sugar

1 teaspoon vanilla bean paste

6 tablespoons superfine sugar

Preheat the oven to 325 degrees. Place six 6-ounce shallow ramekins on a rimmed baking sheet. Set a kettle of water on the stove to boil.

In a small bowl whisk the egg yolks until smooth. Combine the heavy cream and granulated sugar in a medium-sized saucepan and simmer over low heat, stirring until the sugar dissolves and bubbles start to form on the surface. Remove the pan from the heat and slowly whisk in the egg yolks and vanilla bean paste until well combined. This will keep the yolks from curdling.

Strain the liquid in batches through a fine mesh strainer set over a 2-cup measuring cup. Using a rubber spatula, press down on the strainer to retain as much of the liquid as possible, then pour the strained liquid into the ramekins, dividing it evenly. Set the baking sheet in the oven and carefully pour boiling water into the sheet pan and come halfway up the sides of the ramekins, about 1/2 inch deep. (This will prevent the custard from cracking and drying out.)

Bake about 35 to 40 minutes until the custard in each ramekin is set and the centers move slightly when gently shaken. Remove the ramekins from the oven, being careful not to splash any water into the custard. Set the ramekins on a wire rack to cool for 20 to 30 minutes. Then cover them with plastic wrap and chill for at least 3 hours or up to 2 days.

To serve, remove the ramekins from the refrigerator and evenly cover the top of each of the 6 custards with 1 tablespoon of superfine sugar, gently tipping and shaking each ramekin to ensure the top of the custard is completely covered.

Brown the tops with a handheld kitchen torch, moving it back and forth across the sugar until it melts and bubbles. Continue until the sugar becomes aromatic, turns a deep, rich caramel-brown color, and solidifies into a smooth sheet. Cool the custard for a few minutes, until the topping hardens, then serve immediately.

THE CASE FOR A KITCHEN TORCH

I'm not one for a lot of kitchen gadgets, but to make crème brûlée correctly, you'll need a kitchen torch. People may tell you that you can broil the tops in your broiler, but it's not the same. Even if the only thing you use the torch for is to make crème brûlée, it's a sound investment. It's nearly impossible to get a smooth, crunchy brûlée sugar top in the broiler with no burnt spots. A large part of the allure of crème brûlée is the smooth, cool custard under the hard shell, but you have to broil it so long that the custard starts to warm up.

If you must use your broiler, move the custard straight from the refrigerator to the oven, on the top rack, 2 inches from the broiler. It should take 8 to 10 minutes for the sugar to bubble and brown. To ensure the perfect crust, I like to crack the oven door open and keep a close eye on the sugar for the last minute or two. But you'll want to make this recipe so often that it will make sense to invest in a kitchen torch.

TIRAMISU

Tiramisu is another classic dessert composed of layers of brandy-espresso-soaked cookies, creamy mascarpone, and grated chocolate topped with fluffy, sweetened whipped cream and a dusting of cocoa and confectioners' sugar. Tiramisu never disappoints those with a sweet tooth. If you can't find ladyfinger cookies, shortbread cookies also work. Make sure to soak them long enough for the cookies to absorb the liquid.

MAKES 6 TO 8 SERVINGS

Tiramisu

1 1/4 cup ground coffee, brewed in 2 cups water

1/2 cup sugar

1/4 cup coffee brandy

2 egg yolks

16 ounces mascarpone cheese

6 ounces ladyfinger cookies (about 24 cookies)

4 ounces good-quality semisweet chocolate, grated, plus more for garnish

Whipped Cream Topping

1 cup heavy cream

1/4 teaspoon vanilla bean paste

2 tablespoons confectioners' sugar, plus more for dusting

Cocoa for dusting

For the Tiramisu

Line an 8 1/2 x 4 1/2-inch loaf pan with parchment paper, leaving several inches hanging over each long side.

Pour the hot brewed coffee into a shallow bowl and stir in the sugar and brandy until the sugar dissolves, then allow the mixture to cool.

In a medium-sized bowl whisk the egg yolks and mascarpone. Measure out 1/3 cup of the cooled coffee mixture and whisk into the mascarpone mixture until smooth.

Dip the ladyfingers, one at a time, into the remaining coffee mixture and place them in the loaf pan in a single layer. Soak the cookies long enough to absorb some of the liquid but not so long that they fall apart. Spread the cookie layer with 1/3 of the mascarpone mixture, then 1/3 of the grated chocolate. Repeat the layers two more times, then top with a final layer of dipped ladyfingers. Fold the parchment paper over the top of the pan and refrigerate for at least 6 hours or overnight.

For the Topping

Before serving the tiramisu use a stand mixer with a whisk attachment to whip the heavy cream, vanilla bean paste, and confectioners' sugar about 7 to 8 minutes, until stiff peaks form.

To Assemble the Tiramisu

Remove the tiramisu from the refrigerator. Fold the parchment paper back, invert the pan onto a serving platter, and remove the pan and parchment paper. Using an offset spatula, spread the whipped cream over the top and sides of the dessert, or use a pastry bag with a $1/2$-inch piping tip. Dust the tiramisu with cocoa and confectioners' sugar, then garnish with grated chocolate. Slice and serve immediately. Refrigerate any leftovers and eat within a day or two.

LEMON CURD

I couldn't write an egg cookbook and not include lemon curd. I eat it right off the spoon, but it can also be used as a filling for Cream Puffs (page 222), tarts, doughnuts, or Mixed Berry Meringue Nests (page 247) and spread on toast or muffins as well. You can substitute any citrus fruit for the lemons. To get the ¼ cup of juice, you'll need approximately two lemons, two or three limes, one or two oranges, or half of a grapefruit. You may need to adjust the sugar depending on the sweetness of the fruit. The key to a good lemon curd is to cook it slowly over indirect heat, so making this recipe is a helpful exercise in being patient.

MAKES ABOUT 1 ¼ CUPS

3 eggs

3/4 cup sugar

1/4 cup freshly squeezed citrus juice

1/4 cup (1/2 stick) butter, cut into 1/2-inch cubes, room temperature

In a medium-sized saucepan, bring 2 inches of water to a simmer over medium heat. Add the eggs and sugar to a medium-sized glass bowl and set it over the saucepan, making sure the water doesn't touch the bottom of the bowl. Whisk the eggs and sugar until smooth, then add the citrus juice and whisk to combine. Continue to cook, whisking for several minutes, until the mixture is warmed through. Then add the butter, a few cubes at a time, whisking to incorporate before adding more. Continue whisking until the butter melts.

After the butter has been incorporated, continue whisking until it thickens slightly and coats the back of a spoon. This should take about 20 to 25 minutes. Check the water in the pan every now and then to make sure it doesn't simmer away. Add more if needed. If you have a candy thermometer, the curd should be heated to between 180 and 185 degrees. Once the curd has thickened to the correct consistency, remove the bowl from the heat and pour the curd through a fine mesh strainer set over a glass bowl. Using a rubber spatula, scrape the pan clean and press the remaining curd through the strainer.

Enjoy warm or cool the curd to room temperature. Cover and store leftovers in the refrigerator for 2 to 3 weeks.

VANILLA ICE CREAM

Homemade ice cream is so much fun to make. With this basic vanilla recipe, you can add any combination of flavors to create your own custom varieties. You'll need an ice cream maker, of course, and you also need to chill the insert in advance. But the results make the effort worthwhile.

MAKES ABOUT 1 ½ QUARTS

4 cups milk

2 cups heavy cream

3 tablespoons vanilla bean
   paste

1 ¼ cups sugar

½ teaspoon salt

4 egg yolks

Chill your ice cream maker insert, as indicated in the manufacturer's instructions.

In a medium-sized saucepan simmer the milk and cream over medium-high heat until bubbles begin to form around the edges. Remove the pan from the heat, stir in the vanilla bean paste, and let the liquid cool for 10 minutes.

In a medium-sized bowl whisk the sugar, salt, and egg yolks. Slowly add some of the warm milk mixture to the egg mixture, a ladleful at a time to prevent curdling. Whisk to combine, then pour the egg mixture into the saucepan with the remaining milk mixture.

Return the pan to the stove and cook over medium-low heat, whisking constantly, for 2 to 3 minutes to thoroughly warm the liquid. Remove the pan from the heat and pour the mixture into a large bowl. Use a rubber spatula to scrape the pan clean and make sure all the flecks of vanilla transfer to the bowl. Refrigerate the custard until cooled, at least 1 hour or overnight.

Once the custard is chilled, pour it into your ice cream maker and follow the manufacturer's instructions. (My machine takes about 20 to 30 minutes to reach a soft-serve consistency.) Then transfer the mixture to a loaf pan or other freezer-safe container, cover it with plastic wrap, and freeze the ice cream for several hours until it sets.

MINT WHITE CHOCOLATE ICE CREAM

When fresh mint is overflowing in my garden, it's an excuse to make this ice cream. Steeping the fresh mint in the milk imparts a clean, pungent flavor you can't get from an extract. I prefer to use spearmint in my ice cream, but any mint variety will be tasty. In fact, chocolate mint is a nice substitution.

MAKES ABOUT 1 ½ QUARTS

1 cup fresh mint, plus more for garnish

4 cups milk

2 cups heavy cream

2 teaspoons vanilla bean paste

4 egg yolks

1 ¼ cups sugar

½ teaspoon kosher salt

½ cup chopped white chocolate

Chill your ice cream maker insert, as indicated in the manufacturer's instructions.

Tear the mint leaves or rub them between your fingers to release some of the oils. In a medium-sized saucepan, simmer the milk, cream, and mint over medium-high heat, until bubbles form around the edges. Remove the pan from the heat, stir in the vanilla bean paste, and let the mint steep and the mixture cool for 10 minutes. Then discard the mint.

In a medium-sized bowl whisk the egg yolks, sugar, and salt. Slowly add some of the warm milk mixture to the egg mixture, a ladleful at a time to prevent curdling. Whisk to combine, then pour the egg mixture into the saucepan with the remaining milk mixture.

Return the pan to the stove and cook over medium-low heat for 2 to 3 minutes, whisking constantly, to thoroughly warm the liquid. Remove the pan from the heat and pour the mixture into a large bowl. Use a rubber spatula to scrape the pan clean and make sure all the flecks of vanilla transfer to the bowl. Refrigerate the custard until cooled, at least 1 hour or overnight.

Once the custard is chilled, pour it into your ice cream maker and follow the manufacturer's instructions, adding the chopped white chocolate during the last few minutes of churning. Then transfer the mixture into a loaf pan or other freezer-safe container, cover it with plastic wrap, and freeze it for several hours until it sets. Serve garnished with fresh mint.

ROASTED RHUBARB CLAFOUTIS

This classic French dessert calls for whole pitted cherries enveloped in a pillowy, custard-like batter, but any stone fruit will work, as will apples. I like to use fresh rhubarb from the garden whenever I can, and this recipe is a pleasant change from a strawberry rhubarb pie. If you can't find rhubarb, by all means use the cherries or other fruit. The batter will be thin, like a pancake batter, and the flour should be blended in until the batter is smooth, to keep the clafoutis from becoming tough or chewy. Once baked, the consistency will be similar to a loose pudding but will firm up as it cools, so it will stand up to being sliced and eaten with a fork.

MAKES 8 SERVINGS

Butter for greasing the pie plate
   or skillet
2 cups sliced fresh rhubarb
   ($1/2$- inch slices)
2 tablespoons plus $1/2$ cup sugar,
   divided
$3/4$ cup milk
3 eggs
1 teaspoon vanilla bean paste
$1/2$ teaspoon ground ginger
1 tablespoon butter, melted
$1/2$ cup all-purpose flour
Confectioners' sugar for dusting

Preheat the oven to 350 degrees. Use butter to grease a 9-inch pie plate, skillet, or other oven-safe dish. Sprinkle the rhubarb with 2 tablespoons of sugar, toss to coat, and then arrange the rhubarb in an even layer across the bottom. Bake for 10 minutes while you prepare the batter.

Add the milk, eggs, $1/2$ cup sugar, vanilla bean paste, ginger, and butter to a blender and blend until smooth. Add the flour and pulse until incorporated. Pour the batter over the roasted rhubarb. Set the pan on a rimmed baking sheet to prevent overflow, if necessary.

Bake the clafoutis 30 to 35 minutes, until the edges are set and the top is puffed and golden brown. Remove the clafoutis from the oven and let it cool, then dust with confectioners' sugar. Serve warm if you like more of a pudding consistency or at room temperature for a firmer slice. Cover and refrigerate leftovers.

CHOCOLATE POTS DE CRÈME

Who doesn't love warm cream and chocolate served in individual cups? Surprisingly light, pots de crème are rich, creamy, and silky smooth like a mousse.

MAKES 4 SERVINGS

1 cup heavy cream

1/2 cup milk

3 ounces bittersweet chocolate, coarsely chopped, or chips

1/4 cup sugar

3 egg yolks

1/2 teaspoon vanilla bean paste

1 tablespoon crème de cacao, optional

1 tablespoon cocoa, plus more for dusting

1/4 teaspoon kosher salt

Whipped cream for topping, optional

Confectioners' sugar for dusting

Preheat the oven to 300 degrees. Bring a kettle of water to a boil.

In a medium-sized saucepan, simmer the heavy cream and milk over medium heat until bubbles form on the surface. Remove the pan from the heat and add the chocolate and sugar. Stir to combine, then set aside for a few minutes to let the chocolate melt. Whisk until the melted chocolate is incorporated and the sugar is dissolved.

While the chocolate is melting, in a medium-sized bowl whisk the egg yolks, vanilla bean paste, crème de cacao (if desired), cocoa, and salt until smooth. Slowly add a ladleful of the cream mixture to the egg mixture and whisk to combine, making sure the eggs don't curdle. Whisk between each ladleful to temper the eggs. Then pour the egg mixture into the saucepan with the remaining cream mixture and whisk until fully incorporated. Pour the custard through a fine mesh strainer set over a medium-sized bowl.

Set four 4- or 6-ounce ramekins or small oven-safe containers on a rimmed baking sheet. Use a ladle to divide the custard among the ramekins. Place the baking sheet in the oven, then add hot water until it comes halfway up the sides of the ramekins, about 1/2-inch deep.

Bake the custard until almost set, about 30 minutes. Carefully remove the baking sheet from the oven without splashing water into the ramekins. Place the ramekins on a wire rack until they are cool enough to touch, then remove them from the water bath and cool on the rack.

To serve the pots de crème, top with a dollop of whipped cream, if desired, then dust the tops with confectioners' sugar and cocoa. Cover and refrigerate leftovers.

BLUEBERRY ETON MESS

This seemingly complicated dessert is composed of three easy-to-make components that come together in an elegant way in goblets. All three components can be made in advance and assembled immediately before serving, as the celebratory ending to a dinner party or date. I've taken some liberties with the traditional English Eton mess and use blueberries instead of strawberries, but feel free to substitute any berry.

MAKES 4 SERVINGS

Mini-Meringues

3 egg whites, room temperature

1/4 teaspoon cream of tartar

1/8 teaspoon kosher salt

3/4 cup superfine sugar, sifted

1/2 teaspoon vanilla bean paste

For the Mini-Meringues

Preheat the oven to 200 degrees and line a rimmed baking sheet with parchment paper.

Use a stand mixer with a whisk attachment to beat the egg whites, cream of tartar, and salt on medium speed for 30 to 45 seconds until frothy, then increase the mixer to medium-high speed and beat for 2 to 3 additional minutes, until soft peaks form. While the mixer is still running, add the sugar 1 tablespoon at a time until incorporated, then add the vanilla bean paste. Scrape down the sides of the bowl, then increase the mixer speed to high and beat the meringue 5 to 6 minutes, until stiff, glossy peaks form and the meringue has more than quadrupled in volume. To test the meringue's consistency, rub a little between your fingers. When the sugar has dissolved, the meringue will no longer feel gritty.

Use a rubber spatula to scoop the meringue into a pastry bag with a 1/2-inch round or star tip. Set the pastry bag in a 2-cup measuring cup to hold it steady while you're filling it. Pipe the meringue into quarter-size mounds about 1/2 inch apart on the prepared baking sheet.

Bake the meringues about 90 minutes, until they look dry but aren't browned. Don't open the oven for the first 60 minutes. When the meringues are done, turn off the oven, prop the oven door open with a wooden spoon, and leave the meringues to cool in the oven at least 3 hours or overnight.

2 cups blueberries, fresh or
 frozen, plus more for garnish
3 tablespoons sugar
Grated peel of 1 lemon (about
 1 tablespoon)

Whipped Cream

1 cup heavy cream
2 teaspoons confectioners'
 sugar
2 teaspoons vanilla bean paste

For the Sauce

In a medium-sized saucepan, cook the berries, sugar, and
lemon peel over medium heat for about 10 minutes, stirring
occasionally until the sugar is dissolved, the berries are
starting to burst, and the liquid has thickened. Remove the
pan from the heat and cool.

For the Whipped Cream

Use a stand mixer with a whisk attachment to beat the
heavy cream, confectioners' sugar, and vanilla bean paste
on medium-high about 3 minutes, until soft peaks form.

To Assemble the Dessert

In glass goblets or drinking glasses, layer the meringues,
blueberry sauce, and whipped cream, repeating the layers
two or three times. Reserve several meringues for garnish.
Top with whipped cream and garnish with blueberries and
meringues.

MIXED BERRY MERINGUE NESTS

This elegant-looking dessert is surprisingly easy to make. And I especially love that the meringues can be prepared in advance then assembled at dessert time for a light, refreshing summer treat. The meringue nests can be filled with fresh berries and whipped cream or Lemon Curd, if you're feeling more ambitious.

MAKES 4 SERVINGS

Meringue Nests

3 egg whites, room temperature

1/4 teaspoon cream of tartar

1/8 teaspoon kosher salt

3/4 cup superfine sugar, sifted

1 1/2 teaspoons vanilla bean
    paste, divided

2 cups fresh mixed berries
    (blueberries, raspberries,
    blackberries)

3 teaspoons granulated sugar,
    divided

1/2 cup heavy cream

1 1/2 teaspoons vanilla bean
    paste, divided

Fresh thyme sprig or basil leaves
    for garnish

Lemon Curd filling, optional
    (page 236)

Preheat the oven to 200 degrees and line a rimmed baking sheet with parchment paper.

Use a stand mixer with a whisk attachment to beat the egg whites, cream of tartar, and salt on medium-high speed 2 to 3 minutes, until soft peaks form. While the mixer is still running, add the superfine sugar 1 tablespoon at a time until incorporated, then add 1 teaspoon of vanilla bean paste. Scrape down the sides of the bowl, then increase the mixer speed to high and beat the meringue 5 to 6 minutes, until stiff, glossy peaks form and the meringue has more than quadrupled in volume. To test the meringue's consistency, rub a little between your fingers. When the sugar has dissolved, the meringue will no longer feel gritty.

Use a rubber spatula to scoop the meringue into a pastry bag with a large star tip. Set the pastry bag in a 2-cup measuring cup to hold it steady while you're filling it. Pipe the meringue onto the prepared baking sheet in four 4-inch circles, starting in the center of each circle. Then pipe a ring on top outer edge of each circle to create a nest.

Bake the meringues about 90 minutes until they look dry but aren't browned. Don't open the oven for the first 60 minutes. When the meringues are done, turn off the oven, prop the oven door open with a wooden spoon, and leave the meringues to cool in the oven at least 3 hours or overnight.

To Assemble the Nests

To serve the meringue nests, in a medium-sized bowl sprinkle the berries with 2 teaspoons of the granulated sugar then macerate for 30 minutes.

Use a stand mixer with a whisk attachment to beat the heavy cream, the $1/2$ teaspoon of vanilla bean paste, and the remaining teaspoon of granulated sugar on medium-high about 3 minutes, until soft peaks form.

Fill the nests with whipped cream or lemon curd, then top with the berries and garnish with fresh thyme or basil.

SAVE YOUR YOLKS!

Although this recipe calls for only egg whites, remember that you can save the yolks for later use. Lightly whisk the yolks in a bowl, then add a pinch of salt to prevent them from getting gritty after freezing. Coat an ice cube tray with cooking spray, fill each compartment with 1 tablespoon of the yolk mixture, and place the tray in the freezer, where the yolks can be saved for at least six months. See "Freezing Eggs" beginning on page 36 for more information.

You can also use the yolks to make Lemon Curd (page 236) as a filling for the meringue nests.

CONDIMENTS, SAUCES, FILLINGS & TOPPINGS

Let no egg go to waste

If you have your own chickens, you may find yourself collecting more eggs than you can possibly whip into a scramble or fold into an omelet. Even if you don't raise chickens, you'll likely end up with extra eggs you need to eat before they go bad. This is an opportune time to find other ways to use up your stash. This collection of recipe odds and ends should help. Since some of the recipes call for only whites, and others call for only yolks, you can use extra eggs or frozen leftovers from other recipes to make your own condiments and sauces. Separated eggs last about three days in the refrigerator and six months to a year in the freezer.

Mayonnaise, frosting, sweet and savory sauces, and staples like puddings and salad dressings all use eggs. And if you want to have some real fun, try making your own marshmallow crème or sprinkles!

EGG YOLKS

Homemade Mayonnaise
Lemon Caper Garlic Mayonnaise
Spicy Sriracha Mayonnaise
Tartar Sauce
Aioli
Caesar Dressing
Hollandaise Sauce
Béarnaise Sauce
Sabayon
Vanilla Pastry Cream
Crème Anglaise
Vanilla Pudding
Browned Butter Vanilla Cream Pudding

EGG WHITES

Mini-Meringues
Homemade Marshmallows
Marshmallow Crème
Swiss Meringue Buttercream Frosting
Royal Icing
Homemade Sprinkles

HOMEMADE MAYONNAISE

Making homemade mayonnaise is surprisingly easy. The secret is to add the oil very slowly, first by the tablespoon, then in a drizzle, to allow it to emulsify with the egg and other ingredients. And while you can use any cooking oil, a more neutral one—canola, corn, safflower, or sunflower—will let the flavors of the other ingredients come through.

This recipe makes a rich-tasting, thick mayonnaise for sandwiches or dipping fries, if you're that kind of person. Which I am. If raw eggs scare you, this probably isn't the recipe for you, but leaving the mayonnaise out at room temperature for twelve to twenty-four hours will allow the acid in the lemon to neutralize any bacteria before serving.

MAKES ABOUT 1 CUP

3 egg yolks, room temperature
1/2 teaspoon stone-ground mustard
Juice from half a lemon (about 1 tablespoon)
1/2 teaspoon kosher salt
1 cup vegetable oil

Place the egg yolks, mustard, lemon juice, and salt in a wide-mouth, pint-size Mason jar (or a regular blender jar). Pulse a few times with an immersion blender to combine. Once the ingredients are combined, slowly add your oil of choice, 1 tablespoon at a time, pulsing until the oil is incorporated with the egg yolks.

After adding about half the oil, slowly drizzle the remaining oil into the jar, pulsing as you pour. The mayonnaise should start to thicken and lighten to a lemon-yellow color. Continue blending until the mayonnaise is a spreadable consistency. Whisk in a little water if it becomes too thick.

Cover the mayonnaise and leave it out on the counter overnight (or up to 24 hours) before. Store leftovers in the refrigerator for up to a week.

DIJONNAISE

Turn that yummy mayo into a Dijonnaise you can slather on a sandwich or hot dog, by adding 2 tablespoons of mustard, 2 teaspoons of water, and 1 teaspoon of sugar to 1/2 cup of mayonnaise and whisking until smooth. Season with a squeeze of fresh lemon juice, salt, and pepper.

LEMON CAPER GARLIC MAYONNAISE

After mastering homemade mayonnaise, you can experiment with flavors and different add-ins. In this variation, the brightness of the lemon, along with the garlic, makes a fantastic dipping sauce for sweet-potato fries or for slathering on a roast beef sandwich. It's also yummy used in egg salad. I prefer tarragon in this recipe, but you can use parsley instead if you're not a fan of tarragon (or can't find it).

MAKES ABOUT ½ CUP

½ cup Homemade Mayonnaise
   (page 253)
1 teaspoon grated lemon peel
1 tablespoon freshly squeezed
   lemon juice
1 tablespoon chopped capers
1 clove garlic, minced
½ teaspoon chopped fresh
   tarragon
Kosher salt
Freshly ground black pepper

Add the mayonnaise, lemon peel, lemon juice, capers, garlic, and tarragon to a small bowl and stir until well combined. Season with salt and pepper. Cover the bowl and refrigerate for several hours to chill and let the flavors mingle. Give the mayonnaise a quick stir before serving. Store leftovers in the refrigerator for up to a week.

SPICY SRIRACHA MAYONNAISE

Some people love to put hot sauce on, well, everything. Then there's everybody else. I'm not a huge fan of super-spicy, so I love this mild sriracha mayonnaise that you can tweak to achieve your own level of desired spiciness. Start with a bit of sriracha, then add more at the end to taste.

MAKES ABOUT ½ CUP

1/2 cup Homemade Mayonnaise
   (page 253)
1 tablespoon sriracha or hot
   sauce, plus more to taste
Juice of half a lime (about
   1 tablespoon)
1/2 teaspoon honey
1/8 teaspoon kosher salt
Chili flakes for garnish, optional

Place the mayonnaise in a small bowl and stir in the sriracha, lime juice, honey, and salt. Taste and add more hot sauce, if desired. Cover and refrigerate for several hours to chill and let the flavors mingle. Give the mayonnaise a quick stir before serving. Garnish with chili flakes, if desired. Store leftovers in the refrigerator for up to a week.

TARTAR SAUCE

When you make your own mayonnaise, you no longer need to buy tartar sauce either. A few added ingredients turn homemade mayo into the creamiest tartar sauce, to dollop on a plate of fish and chips or use as a dunking sauce for shrimp cocktail. But don't stop there—smear some on a burger, tuna fish sandwich, or an egg sandwich. And of course, you can dip your fries or onion rings in it. While a standard tartar sauce calls for cornichons or baby gherkins, you can use any pickles. Also, if you're using a different pickle type, adding fresh tarragon helps mimic the taste of the brined cornichons. Don't have any pickles? Stir in some relish. No tarragon? Dill works well too.

MAKES ABOUT ½ CUP

1/2 cup Homemade Mayonnaise
(page 253)
2 tablespoons minced pickles
1 tablespoon minced capers
1 teaspoon minced onion
1/2 teaspoon minced fresh
tarragon
2 teaspoons fresh lemon juice
2 to 4 drops of hot sauce,
optional

Place the mayonnaise in a small bowl and stir in the pickles, capers, onion, tarragon, and lemon juice until combined. Add the hot sauce to taste. Cover the bowl and chill for several hours to let the flavors mingle. Give the tartar sauce a quick stir before serving. Store leftovers in the refrigerator for up to a week.

AIOLI

Aioli might look like mayonnaise, but it's actually a rich sauce made with garlic and olive oil that's popular in Mediterranean cuisine. Creamy and mouthwatering with aromatic garlic and tart lemon, aioli makes a zesty dipping sauce for fries or veggies, and it can be drizzled over fish, eggs, or pasta.

MAKES ABOUT ¾ CUP

2 garlic cloves

2 egg yolks, room temperature

½ cup extra virgin olive oil

2 tablespoons freshly squeezed lemon juice

Kosher salt

Grate the garlic into a medium-sized bowl with a Microplane or grater. Whisk in the egg yolks until well combined. Slowly drizzle in the oil in a thin stream, whisking constantly, until the mixture emulsifies and thickens. Whisk in the lemon juice and season with salt. Add water to thin the aioli, if necessary. Store leftovers in the refrigerator up to 4 days.

CAESAR DRESSING

I know what you're thinking: *Why should I make my own Caesar dressing when I can easily buy a bottle of it?* I'll tell you why: It's simple to make and far better than store-bought dressing. You can have a batch whipped up in less time than it takes you to find your car keys.

You probably have all the ingredients already on hand, so you owe it to yourself to make your own. At least once. The anchovy paste is optional, but if you can, please give it a try before you decide to omit it. Just a touch gives the dressing a subtle, salty punch.

MAKES ABOUT ¾ CUP

3 egg yolks

2 garlic cloves, roughly chopped

1/2 cup freshly grated Parmesan cheese

2 teaspoons anchovy paste

1 teaspoon stone-ground mustard

Grated peel of 1 lemon (about 1 tablespoon)

Juice of 1 lemon (about 3 tablespoons)

1/2 cup vegetable oil, such as safflower

1 tablespoon water

Kosher salt

Freshly ground black pepper

In a blender or food processor, puree the egg yolks, garlic, Parmesan, anchovy paste, mustard, lemon peel, and lemon juice about 10 seconds, until smooth. Scrape down the sides of the blender with a rubber spatula. Remove the lid insert and, with the blender is still running, slowly drizzle the oil into the mixture until it thickens and the oil is incorporated. Don't rush this step—the oil needs time to emulsify with the eggs. While the blender is still running, add the water slowly until the dressing is a pourable consistency. Season with salt and pepper. Cover and refrigerate any leftovers. Use within 1 or 2 days.

HOLLANDAISE SAUCE

Making traditional hollandaise sauce involves standing over a double broiler on the stove, whisking the butter into the sauce. But blender hollandaise comes together quickly and easily and produces nearly identical results: an extraordinarily stable sauce that holds up and doesn't break. Make sure to add the butter slowly and blend the sauce long enough for it to emulsify and fully combine, and you'll be good to go.

MAKES ABOUT 1 CUP

3 egg yolks

2 tablespoons freshly squeezed lemon juice

1 tablespoon water

1/2 cup (1 stick) butter, cut into 1/2-inch cubes and chilled

Freshly grated nutmeg

Kosher salt

White pepper

Stove-top Method

Bring a small pot of water to a boil. Add the egg yolks, lemon juice, and water to a heatproof glass bowl and set it over the pot of boiling water, making sure the water doesn't touch the bottom of the bowl. Whisk the mixture until combined. Slowly add the butter, a few pieces at a time, whisking continuously until the butter is melted and fully incorporated. Cook the hollandaise sauce for another minute or two, continuing to whisk until it thickens. Season with nutmeg, salt, and pepper. Immediately remove the sauce from the heat and serve.

Blender Method

Add the egg yolks, lemon juice, and water to a blender and pulse 3 to 5 seconds until well mixed. Melt the butter and slowly pour it through the top of the blender while the motor is running. Continue to blend about 30 seconds, until the sauce is light-colored, creamy, and emulsified. Season with nutmeg, salt, and pepper.

Mason Jar Method

Add the egg yolks, lemon juice, and water to a wide-mouth Mason jar. Melt the butter and slowly drizzle over the eggs while mixing with an immersion blender. Continue to blend about 30 seconds, until the sauce is light-colored, creamy, and emulsified. Season with nutmeg, salt, and pepper.

BÉARNAISE SAUCE

Meet the sassy, sophisticated cousin of hollandaise. Buttery and smooth with a kick of vinegar and lemon, béarnaise has a reputation for being difficult to make and breaking easily. But you'll master the technique in no time with the same foolproof blender method used to make hollandaise sauce. Clarifying the butter is an optional but important step, since it removes milk solids and water from the butter, resulting in a smoother, richer sauce. The sauce is best used immediately, so blend it up last when preparing your meal.

MAKES ABOUT ¾ CUP

1 cup (2 sticks) butter

¼ cup champagne vinegar

3 tablespoons chopped shallots

2 tablespoons chopped fresh
tarragon, plus more for
garnish

¼ teaspoon freshly ground
black pepper

2 egg yolks, room temperature

Juice of half a lemon (about
1 tablespoon)

1 tablespoon water, room
temperature

Kosher salt

To clarify the butter, melt it in a small saucepan over low heat. Remove the pan from the heat and let the butter cool for 4 to 5 minutes. Use a spoon to carefully skim the foam off the top of the butter and discard. Slowly pour the liquid into a measuring cup, discarding the milky solids in the bottom of the saucepan.

In a medium-sized skillet over medium-low heat, simmer the vinegar, shallots, tarragon, and pepper for 2 to 3 minutes, stirring occasionally until the liquid is reduced by half. Remove the pan from the heat and cool slightly.

Using a blender, puree the egg yolks, lemon juice, and water until smooth. Remove the lid insert and slowly pour a thin stream of the melted butter into the blender while the motor is running. As with mayonnaise, adding the butter too quickly can cause the sauce to separate or "break," so don't rush this step. Continue to blend until the sauce is smooth and creamy. Add more water if the sauce is too thick. It should be pourable—like the consistency of thick eggnog.

Pour the sauce into a medium-sized bowl, stir in the shallot mixture, and season with salt. Garnish with tarragon and use immediately.

SABAYON

Sabayon is a sweet dessert sauce made by whisking egg yolks, sugar, and a sweet table or dessert wine over a double boiler. Marsala wine is standard, but this recipe can use vermouth, sherry, brandy, amaretto, or any dessert wine of your choice. Best poured over fresh berries, sabayon is a French recipe, although an Italian version called zabaglione is similar. No matter where it originated, this sauce is easy to master and makes an ordinary bowlful of fresh berries sing. In late summer, I love to pour sabayon over freshly picked berries. Any type of berries work in this recipe, but I prefer a combination of strawberries, raspberries, blackberries, and blueberries.

MAKES 4 SERVINGS

4 egg yolks
4 tablespoons superfine sugar
4 tablespoons marsala wine
3 cups fresh berries, for serving

Bring a pot of water to a simmer over medium heat. Add the egg yolks and sugar to a medium heatproof glass bowl and set over the pot. Whisk the mixture until well combined, then slowly pour in the marsala, whisking constantly. Keep whisking about 7 to 8 minutes, while the sauce cooks and thickens to a mousse-like but still pourable consistency.

Remove the sauce from the heat and continue whisking for a few minutes until the sabayon is slightly warmer than room temperature. Divide the berries among 4 dessert bowls and spoon or pour the sauce on top.

VANILLA PASTRY CREAM

Pastry cream is similar to pudding or custard, but thanks to more eggs, it's richer and thicker. Because of this, it pipes well and can be used to fill Cream Puffs (page 222), eclairs, or a Boston Cream Pie (page 198).

MAKES ABOUT 3 CUPS

6 egg yolks, room temperature

1/2 cup sugar

2 tablespoons all-purpose flour

2 tablespoons cornstarch

1/8 teaspoon kosher salt

1 cup milk

1 cup heavy cream

2 teaspoons vanilla bean paste

1 tablespoon butter

In a medium-sized bowl whisk the egg yolks, sugar, flour, cornstarch, and salt until smooth.

In a medium-heavy saucepan warm the milk and cream over medium heat until the edges start to bubble. Remove the pan from the heat and slowly spoon a few ladlefuls of the hot milk mixture into the egg mixture, whisking vigorously to temper the egg yolks so they don't curdle. Pour the egg mixture into the pan and continue to cook over low heat for 3 to 4 minutes, whisking constantly, until the mixture is bubbly and thick. Remove the pan from the heat and whisk in the vanilla bean paste and butter. Continue whisking until the butter melts and is incorporated.

Transfer the pastry cream to a medium-sized bowl and press plastic wrap over the surface to prevent a skin from forming. Let the cream cool to room temperature, then refrigerate for at least 2 hours before using.

CRÈME ANGLAISE

This light, pourable custard goes wonderfully over pies, cakes, or berries. You can serve it chilled or at room temperature to add a richness to a variety of desserts. I especially love crème anglaise poured over pancakes, bread pudding, or a slice of pound cake.

MAKES ABOUT 1 CUP

2 egg yolks

3 tablespoons sugar

1/2 cup milk

1/2 cup heavy cream

2 teaspoons vanilla bean paste

In a medium-sized bowl whisk the egg yolks and sugar until smooth.

In a medium-sized saucepan warm the milk, cream, and vanilla bean paste over medium-high heat, whisking occasionally until the liquid starts to bubble around the edges. Be careful not to let the milk boil or scald. Remove the pan from the heat and slowly pour a few spoonfuls of the milk mixture into the egg mixture, whisking to combine. Add several more spoonfuls, whisking between each spoonful so the eggs don't curdle.

Pour the egg mixture into the saucepan and whisk constantly over low heat about 2 to 3 minutes until it thickens to a pourable consistency. The custard should be slightly thicker than heavy cream, coat the back of a spoon, and leave a trail when you run your finger down the spoon.

Remove the pan from the heat and pour the custard through a fine mesh strainer set over a glass bowl. Use a rubber spatula to scrape the pan clean and press the custard through the strainer to make sure all those beautiful flecks of vanilla transfer to the bowl. Cool the custard to room temperature before serving. Cover and store leftovers in the refrigerator for 3 to 4 days.

VANILLA PUDDING

Here's a quick, basic pudding recipe that you can stuff in doughnuts, use as a cupcake filling, or eat straight from the bowl. Make this recipe once, and you'll swear off boxed mixes forever. Typically, custards are thickened with eggs, and puddings are thickened with cornstarch or flour, but this recipe uses both to achieve a firm, silky, creamy consistency. The pudding isn't as thick as pastry cream, so it won't hold its shape as a piped decoration, but it still can be used either as a filling or a stand-alone dessert.

MAKES ABOUT 2 CUPS

2 cups milk

2 egg yolks

1/3 cup firmly packed light brown sugar

3 tablespoons cornstarch

Kosher salt

1/2 teaspoon vanilla bean paste

In a medium-sized saucepan whisk the milk and egg yolks over medium heat until combined. Add the brown sugar, cornstarch, and salt, and continue whisking 5 to 6 minutes until the pudding thickens and starts bubbling.

Remove the pan from the heat and whisk in the vanilla bean paste. Pour the pudding through a fine mesh strainer set over a glass bowl. Use a spoon or rubber spatula to scrape the pan clean and press the custard through the strainer.

Serve warm or cover the bowl with plastic wrap, pressing the wrap over the surface of the pudding to prevent a skin from forming, and chill for at least 2 hours. To serve, remove the plastic wrap and whisk the pudding until it's smooth.

BROWNED BUTTER VANILLA CREAM PUDDING

A variation of my basic vanilla pudding recipe, this decadent pudding substitutes heavy cream for the milk and calls for browning the butter before swirling it into the finished pudding.

2 cups heavy cream

2 egg yolks

1/3 cup firmly packed light brown sugar

3 tablespoons cornstarch

Kosher salt

1/2 teaspoon vanilla bean paste

2 tablespoons butter

Whipped cream for serving, optional

Turbinado sugar for garnish

In a medium-sized saucepan whisk the cream and egg yolks over medium heat. Add the brown sugar, cornstarch, and salt and continue whisking 5 to 6 minutes until the pudding thickens and starts bubbling.

Remove the pan from the heat and whisk in the vanilla bean paste. Pour the pudding through a fine mesh strainer set over a glass bowl. Use a spoon or rubber spatula to scrape the pan clean and press the custard through the strainer. Set aside to cool.

Melt the butter in a small frying pan over medium-low heat and cook 2 to 3 minutes, whisking occasionally until the butter begins to brown and smells nutty. Pour the butter into the pudding and whisk until incorporated.

Serve the pudding warm or cover the bowl with plastic wrap, pressing the wrap over the surface of the pudding to prevent a skin from forming, and chill for at least 2 hours. To serve, remove the plastic wrap and whisk the pudding until it's smooth. Top with whipped cream and turbinado sugar, if desired.

MINI-MERINGUES

Meringues are super-easy, albeit finicky (which is why I've included some handy notes to help you out!). These light and airy little cookies can be served on their own or to garnish other desserts. They're crispy on the outside, but the insides should melt in your mouth. I flavor mine with vanilla, but you can add any flavoring you wish, or food coloring for that matter. This is a good, basic recipe that can be adapted in lots of different ways.

MAKES ABOUT 4 DOZEN

3 egg whites, room temperature
1/4 teaspoon cream of tartar
1/8 teaspoon kosher salt
3/4 cup superfine sugar, sifted
1/2 teaspoon vanilla bean paste

Preheat the oven to 200 degrees and line a rimmed baking sheet with parchment paper.

Use a stand mixer with a whisk attachment to beat the egg whites, cream of tartar, and salt on medium for 30 to 45 seconds until frothy, then increase the speed to medium-high speed for 1 to 2 minutes, until soft peaks form. While the mixer is still running, add the sugar 1 tablespoon at a time until incorporated, then add the vanilla bean paste. Scrape down the sides of the bowl, then increase the mixer speed to high and beat the meringue 5 to 6 minutes, until stiff, glossy peaks form and the meringue has more than quadrupled in volume. To test the meringue's consistency, rub a little between your fingers. When the sugar has dissolved, the meringue will no longer feel gritty.

Using a rubber spatula, scoop the meringue into a pastry bag with a 1/2-inch round or star tip. Set the pastry bag in a 2-cup measuring cup to hold it steady while you're filling it.

Pipe the meringue into quarter-size mounds about 1/2 inch apart on the prepared baking sheet. Bake the meringues about 90 minutes, until they look dry but aren't browned. Don't open the oven for the first 60 minutes. When the meringues are done, turn the oven off, prop the oven door open with a wooden spoon, and leave the meringues in the oven to cool at least 3 hours or overnight.

Store the meringues in an airtight container for up to 2 weeks or freeze for later use.

MERINGUE TIPS

- Don't make meringues on a rainy, damp, or humid day. The drier the air the better.

- Make sure your eggs are at room temperature. Cold eggs separate more easily than warm eggs, so separate each egg right from the refrigerator. Then let the whites sit out on the counter for about 30 minutes to come to room temperature.

- If you don't have any superfine sugar, briefly whirl an equal amount of granulated sugar in a coffee grinder or food processor to pulverize it. The finer your sugar, the less gritty your meringues will be.

- Make sure the mixing bowl and whisk are squeaky clean—a single speck of grease or fat (think egg yolk!) will prevent the meringue from whipping up correctly.

- Mix the sugar on medium speed until all of it has been incorporated, then turn up the mixer speed to high.

- No peeking! Don't open the oven door until the meringues have baked for at least 60 minutes—and preferably the entire time.

HOMEMADE MARSHMALLOWS

If you've never tried making homemade marshmallows, get ready to be delighted. You can make plain vanilla or add another extract and food coloring. Either way, these marshmallows are easy to make, but be aware they'll need to sit for several hours to dry out enough to cut, so start first thing in the morning if you want to serve them for dessert or pop them into a cup of hot cocoa in the evening. The yield will depend on how large you cut the marshmallows.

MAKES 3 TO 6 DOZEN

1 cup confectioners' sugar, divided, plus more for dusting

1 1/2 cups water, divided

4 tablespoons unflavored gelatin powder

2 cups granulated sugar

1 tablespoon light corn syrup

2 egg whites, room temperature

1 teaspoon vanilla bean paste

Sift 1/4 cup of the confectioners' sugar to evenly cover the bottom of a 9-inch square baking pan.

Pour 3/4 cup of water into a small glass bowl and sprinkle the gelatin over the top. Set the bowl over a small pot of simmering water to allow the gelatin to dissolve, then whisk to combine. Turn off the heat and leave the bowl in place.

In a medium-sized saucepan stir the granulated sugar, corn syrup, and remaining 3/4 cup of water over medium-high heat until combined. Without stirring, heat the mixture to 245 degrees, using a candy thermometer to monitor the temperature.

Use a stand mixer with a whisk attachment to beat the egg whites on medium for 30 to 45 seconds until frothy, then increase the mixer speed to medium-high and beat for 1 to 2 minutes, until soft peaks form.

When the syrup reaches 245 degrees, remove it from the heat and slowly whisk in the dissolved gelatin mixture until combined. With the mixer set to low, slowly pour the syrup mixture into the egg whites, to temper them so they won't curdle. Increase the mixer speed to medium-high and continue to whip 5 to 6 minutes, until the mixture has at least doubled in size and the bowl is no longer hot.

Add the vanilla bean paste and whisk until combined. Using a rubber spatula, scoop the marshmallow mixture evenly into the prepared pan. Sift another 1/4 cup of confectioners' sugar over the top.

Let the marshmallow batter rest on the counter for 6 to 8 hours (or overnight) before cutting. To serve, run a butter knife along the outer edge of the pan to loosen the marshmallow block. Turn the block out of the pan onto a work surface dusted with confectioners' sugar. Rub the blades of a pair of kitchen shears with confectioners' sugar, then cut the marshmallow into 1- to 1 1/2-inch squares for regular or jumbo marshmallows. Toss the squares in the remaining 1/2 cup of confectioners' sugar to prevent them from sticking together. Store the marshmallows in an airtight container at room temperature for up to a week.

Flavored Marshmallows

I'm a big fan of natural and plant-based food colorings and love to make pale-purple, blackberry-flavored marshmallows with blackberry extract and blue and red natural food coloring. Feel free to experiment with other flavors and colors as well.

1/2 teaspoon blackberry extract
Red and blue plant-based food coloring

Follow the instructions for making homemade marshmallows, then after adding the vanilla bean paste, add the extract and food coloring until your mixture is the desired tint. Continue with the remaining instructions.

MARSHMALLOW CRÈME

I don't think you can grow up in New England—or Massachusetts specifically, where Marshmallow Fluff originated—and not run into a fluffernutter sandwich. A lunch staple for many children, the ooey-gooey marshmallow crème not only pairs well with peanut butter but also makes a wonderful filling or frosting for cakes and cupcakes. Surprisingly easy to make, once you've tried this recipe you'll never go back to store bought (isn't that always the case?), and you'll discover the magic of the fluffernutter sandwich. The fluff is also a wonderful addition to my Peanut Butter and Jelly Cookie Sandwiches (page 218).

MAKES ABOUT 3 CUPS

1/3 cup water

3/4 cup sugar

3/4 cup white corn syrup

3 egg whites, room temperature

1/2 teaspoon cream of tartar

1 1/2 teaspoons vanilla bean paste

In a medium-sized saucepan combine the water, sugar, and corn syrup over medium-high heat. Without stirring, heat the syrup to 240 degrees, using a candy thermometer to monitor the temperature. This should take about 10 minutes.

While the syrup is heating, use a stand mixer with a whisk attachment to beat the eggs whites and cream of tartar on medium for 30 to 45 seconds until frothy, then increase the mixer speed to medium-high and beat for 1 to 2 minutes, until soft peaks form. (Make sure the bowl is free of grease and yolk specks, or your whites won't whip.)

When the syrup reaches 240 degrees, remove the pan from the heat and with the stand mixer set to medium-low, slowly pour the syrup into the egg whites, to temper the whites so they won't curdle. Increase the mixer speed to medium-high and continue to whip the mixture about 7 to 8 minutes, until the whites thicken and turn glossy. Scrape down the sides of the bowl as needed. Add the vanilla bean paste and whip until combined. Scrape down the sides of the bowl one last time.

Use a rubber spatula to scoop the crème into a covered container and store in the refrigerator for up to 2 weeks. Before serving, rewhip by hand, if needed.

SWISS MERINGUE BUTTERCREAM FROSTING

There are several different types of buttercream frosting, but this Swiss meringue is my most loved. It's fairly easy to make and results in a spreadable, pipeable frosting that's not too sweet and can easily be flavored with extracts, chocolate (a variation I provide with this recipe), peanut butter, or fruit jams—or colored with food coloring.

MAKES 5 TO 6 CUPS

6 egg whites

1 1/2 cups superfine sugar

2 1/2 cups (5 sticks) butter, cut into 1/2-inch cubes, room temperature

2 teaspoons vanilla bean paste

Pinch of kosher salt

Bring a small saucepan of water to a simmer over medium heat. Whisk the egg whites and sugar by hand in the bowl of a stand mixer set over the saucepan. Heat the mixture to 160 to 165 degrees, whisking occasionally and using a candy thermometer to monitor the temperature. To test the mixture's consistency, rub a little between your fingers. When it's no longer gritty, set the bowl on the stand mixer with a whisk attachment and beat on high speed about 10 minutes, until stiff peaks form and the bowl is no longer warm.

Switch to a paddle attachment and add the butter a few cubes at a time, beating well to incorporate before adding more. Reduce the mixer speed to low and beat in the vanilla bean paste and salt for 2 to 3 minutes, until the frosting is fluffy and smooth, scraping down the sides of the bowl as needed. (At this point, mix in any extra flavorings or food coloring you want to include.)

Use the frosting immediately to frost a 2-layer cake or 12 cupcakes, or to fill 1 jelly roll. Otherwise, refrigerate for up to 3 days. Before using chilled frosting, bring it to room temperature and whip to fluff it up.

Chocolate Buttercream

Make the buttercream frosting as directed, and at the point you add flavorings, mix 6 ounces of melted, good-quality semisweet chocolate into the frosting, until all the streaks are gone. The chocolate should be cool but still pourable, so it doesn't loosen up the frosting.

ROYAL ICING

If you've ever drooled over perfectly decorated cookies or a pristine gingerbread house in a bakery window or on Pinterest or Instagram, chances are that the baker used royal icing to make them. Royal icing dries to a smooth, hard finish for professional results every time. It's another great way to use extra egg whites. The addition of lemon juice makes the icing pure white, or you can create custom colors with food coloring. The key is to keep the mixer on medium speed, to prevent excess air—and bubbles—from being incorporated into the icing as it's being mixed.

MAKES ABOUT 3 CUPS

3 egg whites
4 cups confectioners' sugar
1 teaspoon fresh lemon juice
Food coloring, optional

Use a stand mixer with a paddle attachment to beat the eggs whites on low speed about 1 minute, until foamy. Gradually sift the confectioners' sugar into the egg whites, continuing to beat the mixture, then add the lemon juice. Increase the mixer speed to medium and beat 5 to 7 minutes, until stiff peaks form.

Cover the icing with a damp towel and let it sit for a few minutes, then run a knife through it to remove any air bubbles. Using a rubber spatula, scrape the icing into a bowl (or bowls) and add food coloring as desired. Cover with the damp towel while decorating cookies so the icing doesn't dry out. Stir in a little water to thin the icing, if necessary.

Royal icing should dry to the touch in 15 to 20 minutes, but let frosted cookies sit uncovered overnight to dry. Store extra icing in an airtight container for up to 3 days.

HOMEMADE SPRINKLES

When you live in a remote area, there's no such thing as a quick trip to the grocery store. So one summer afternoon, our rural lifestyle led me to google how to make homemade sprinkles. Sprinkles make people smile, and while making them yourself is a bit time consuming and labor intensive, I was grinning as I showed my husband my first batch. Kids will love making them, so get them involved too!

MAKES ABOUT ½ CUP

2 cups confectioners' sugar

1 egg white

1 teaspoon water

Assorted extract flavors

Food coloring drops or gel

Line 2 rimmed baking sheets with parchment paper.

Sift the sugar into a medium-sized bowl, then using a rubber spatula, stir in the egg white. Slowly add the water a few drops at a time, stirring to form a sticky paste the consistency of liquid glue or runny toothpaste.

Keep the dough in the bowl covered with a kitchen towel while you work with 1 color/flavor at a time. Spoon a generous tablespoon of dough into a small bowl. Add several drops of extract (almond, lemon, orange, raspberry, and blackberry flavors are all great options) and a corresponding food color, then knead the dough with the spatula or your fingers until it's smooth and the color is incorporated. Tint the dough slightly darker than you want the final sprinkles to be, since the color will fade as they dry.

Fit a pastry bag with a #3 piping tip and scrape the dough into the bag. Then pipe the dough into thin parallel lines on the parchment paper, ¼-inch apart.

Repeat 5 more times for a total of 6 colors/flavors, leaving one batch untinted (I like to flavor the white batch with vanilla bean paste).

Let your piped lines of dough dry for at least 3 to 4 hours, then once they are dry to the touch, carefully cut them into ¼-inch lengths with a sharp knife. Use a spatula to slide the sprinkles off the parchment paper onto a plate. Let them dry uncovered overnight, then store in an airtight container for up to a month.

ADDITIONAL RESOURCES

PANTRY AND KITCHEN INGREDIENTS

The ingredients I stock tend to be simple and easy to find, but high end, and I think they're worth the expense. With a splash of champagne vinegar, a drizzle of truffle oil, a few capers, or a vanilla bean, you can elevate basic ingredients to restaurant-quality meals. I keep several types of La Tourangelle cooking oil on hand. Using truffle, sesame, avocado, peanut, or walnut oil in a dish can drastically improve the flavor.

Whenever possible, I try to use locally sourced products, buying from farmers markets or choosing local brands at the grocery store. I use Vermont-based King Arthur flour, butter from the Cabot Creamery dairy cooperative of New England family farms, heavy cream and whole milk from Oakhurst Dairy right here in Maine, and Wyman's frozen Maine blueberries when I can't get fresh berries from a local blueberry farm. We buy apples from an orchard not far from our house and pick strawberries at another local farm when they're in season. And our maple syrup comes from a sugar shack we visit on Maine Maple Sunday. As for eggs, if you don't have your own chickens, try tracking some farm-fresh eggs down at a farmers market or roadside stand, or check your grocery store for a local farm or co-op brand. Buying locally helps support our friends and neighbors and ensures that we're getting the freshest, best-quality meats, dairy, and produce possible.

Here's what you might commonly find in my kitchen and pantry on any given day:

REFRIGERATOR

Eggs	Salted and unsalted butter	Swiss cheese
Fresh berries	Mayonnaise	Parmesan cheese
Active dry yeast	Cream cheese	Ricotta cheese
Maple syrup	Cheddar cheese	Capers
Milk	Fontina cheese	Stone-ground mustard
Heavy cream	Gruyère cheese	

FREEZER

Walnuts	Limes	Fresh ginger
Pecans	Lemons	Frozen berries
Pistachios	Puff pastry	Frozen rhubarb

KITCHEN COUNTER

More eggs	Garlic	Scallions
Potted herbs		

PANTRY

All-purpose flour	Superfine sugar	Extra-virgin olive oil
00 pasta flour	Confectioners' sugar	Various cooking oils
Almond flour	Cocoa	Balsamic vinegar
Baking powder	Chocolate chips	Champagne vinegar
Baking soda	White chocolate chips	Honey
Bakewell cream	Almond paste or marzipan	Molasses
Granulated sugar	Peanut butter	
Brown sugar	Dried pasta	

SPICES

Black peppercorns	Maldon sea salt	Nutmeg (whole in a grinder)
Green peppercorns	Cardamom	Vanilla bean paste
White peppercorns	Chai spice	Vanilla beans
Pink peppercorns	Ground cinnamon	Sesame seeds
Kosher salt	Cinnamon sticks	Assorted sprinkles
Pink Himalayan salt	Ginger	

FROM MY FARM AND KITCHEN GARDEN

Raspberries
Blueberries
Rhubarb
Strawberries
Crab apples
Peas

Green beans
Radishes
Beets
Cucumbers
Spinach
Lettuce

Corn
Eggplant
Garlic
Onions
Sweet potatoes
Tomatoes

KITCHEN UTENSILS AND APPLIANCES

Despite cooking at least one meal from scratch every day, in addition to being an avid baker and attempting techniques like brûlée and meringue, I don't own many kitchen appliances, and I try to keep my utensils in check.

I'm not a fan of large machines or gadgets that only do one thing (except for a kitchen torch!). I don't even own a bread machine anymore, since I learned to bake bread in a Dutch oven.

However, one appliance I swear by is my KitchenAid stand mixer. I've had mine since my early twenties, and it shows no signs of slowing down. It not only whips and beats any number of ingredients but also makes ice cream and pasta, as well as a decent pizza crust and bread dough.

Along with my stand mixer, I own an array of baking pans, because cakes like angel food need to be made in a specific pan, and a tart pan and springform pan with removable bottoms are invaluable. Cupcake or muffin tins are another essential. Popover pans are fun to have but definitely a luxury.

All that said, some appliances and utensils are essential to every kitchen and make life easier if you're a frequent cook/baker. And of course you'll need a set of knives. You don't need more than a few knives, as long as they're sharp and high quality. A chef's knife and paring knife are what I reach for most often, as well as a serrated knife to cut bread and tomatoes.

You'll also reach for some standard pots and pans in your day-to-day kitchen adventures. Pans come in various sizes, so choose the size that makes the most sense for you, depending on the number of people you generally cook for.

Here's a rundown of the utensils and appliances I keep in my kitchen drawers and cabinets:

ESSENTIAL UTENSILS

Wooden spoons
Rubber spatulas
Metal spatula
Offset spatula
Cake slicer
Tongs
Whisks, small and large
Measuring spoons
Measuring cups, wet and dry
Mise en place bowls
Ice cream scoop
Rolling pin
Pastry brush

Pastry cutter
Bench scraper
Round biscuit or cookie cutter
Colander
Fine mesh strainer/sifter
Ladle
Slotted spoon
Pie weights
Vegetable peeler
Grater
Microplane
Hand juicer
Kitchen shears

POTS AND PANS

Frying pans or skillets, medium and large
Small saucepan
Dutch oven
Stock pot with lid
13 x 18 x 1-inch rimmed baking sheets
Round 8- or 9-inch cake pans
Square 8- or 9-inch cake pans
Casserole dish
Bundt pan

Tube pan
Tart pan with removable bottom
Springform pan
Popover pan
Pie plate
Cupcake/muffin tins
Ramekins
Mixing bowls, large and small

APPLIANCES

Stand mixer
Hand mixer
Blender
Immersion blender
Food processor

Ice cream maker
Coffee bean grinder
Toaster
Manual pasta machine

MISCELLANEOUS

Cutting board
Wire cooling racks
Parchment paper
Aluminum foil
Plastic wrap

Cupcake papers
Cheesecloth
Pastry cloth
Pastry bag and piping tips

CARING FOR YOUR CAST-IRON SKILLET

I'm not a fan of nonstick pans, and I swear by a cast-iron skillet. Like my grandmother, I can (and do!) cook almost anything in cast-iron. Acidic foods can pit the surface, so I don't let tomato sauce sit in the pan for any length of time. And if you're planning on making many omelets, adding a more lightweight skillet with sloped sides is a must for your arsenal.

But seasoned properly, a cast-iron skillet will perform as well as any nonstick pan and has the added benefit of being able to go from the stove top to the oven without a problem. Stainless steel or copper pots are pretty, but I prefer cast-iron or enamel for their nonstick properties and ability to use less fat in the pan. My current favorites are my enameled cast-iron skillets and pans.

Whether you inherited your great-grandmother's cast-iron skillet, picked one up at a yard sale, or purchased yours brand new, cast-iron does require some maintenance to perform at its very best.

New skillets will come preseasoned. A well-seasoned cast-iron skillet shouldn't need much oil, butter, or grease, if any, to prevent foods from sticking when you cook. As long as you heat the pan before adding your meats, eggs, or veggies, you should find the cast-iron skillets cook and sear well without sticking.

Caring for your cast-iron skillet is essential. It should always be washed by hand, never in the dishwasher. It should not be soaked or left with water sitting in it. And you should *never* use soap in your skillet! Normally, a quick scrub with a scratchy sponge will be all it takes to remove food residue from your skillet, then a rinse in hot water. You can also use steel wool for stubborn bits of food that are burned onto cast-iron skillets (never scrub your enamaled pans!). Or generously sprinkle salt into a still-warm skillet and rub the food debris away using a sponge or kitchen towel.

After the inside of the skillet is clean and free of any debris, wipe the inside with a paper towel to dry it. My father-in-law would instead set the skillet back on the still-warm stove or on a burner with the flame turned as low as it would go to dry the inside quickly and evaporated every last bit of moisture. When your skillet is dry, a quick rub of olive oil or coconut oil on the inside is all it needs to maintain the seasoning.

If you run across an old, rusted cast-iron pan at a yard sale or antique store, don't hesitate to buy it! Bring it home, scrub it with steel wool, then season it with oil. If an old skillet needs some TLC, rub the inside generously with oil, then put it in an oven on low (300 to 350 degrees) for an hour. When the skillet is seasoned, remove it from the oven, let it cool, then wipe off any excess oil with a paper towel, and your skillet should be good as new.

ACKNOWLEDGMENTS

A heartfelt thank you to everyone who made my dream of writing a cookbook a reality. Thanks to my agent, John Maas, for somehow understanding the essence of my original vision, which existed only in my head, and for helping me whip it into shape (pun intended!). Thank you to Andrea Fleck-Nisbet, publisher; Amanda Bauch, senior editor; and the rest of the Harper Horizon team for sharing that vision, believing in me, and then having the patience to guide me through this entire cookbook-writing process, which was brand new to me. Without you, this book would not have been possible. Thanks to fellow cookbook author Anne Byrn for your guidance and for gently nudging me in the right direction throughout the process and organizing my very scattered rough draft. Thank you to photographer Tina Rupp (I'm still pinching myself that you agreed to take on this project!), who made my recipes look far more mouthwatering than I ever could. And thank you to Cyd McDowell, who styled everything so beautifully and taught me how to make the perfect whipped cream dollop— *kiitos!* To Mimi and Star—those two weeks wouldn't have been the same without you both. Let's do it again sometime. A huge thank you to my husband, Mark, who not only ate way more eggs on demand than he likely wanted to, but who always steps in to take care of the chickens when I'm not around. Thank you to my mom for a million things, of course, but mostly for teaching me how to cook when I was so small I had to stand on a kitchen chair to see over the stove top. And lastly, thank you to my chickens. I think we all know why.

RECIPE INDEX

BY NUMBER OF EGGS NEEDED

Since the number of fresh eggs you have on hand throughout the year might vary, this index is intended to help you find a use for them all. If a recipe requires a combination of whole eggs and/or whites and yolks, or only whites or yolks, this is indicated in parentheses following the recipe title. Fresh eggs are too precious—and the chickens work way too hard to lay each one—to let a single egg go to waste!

1 EGG

Blueberry Cobbler
Egg Flip
French Toast
Homemade Sprinkles (1 white)
Lime Bourbon Sour (1 white)
Maple Sour (1 white)
Pecan Pumpkin Spice Pancakes
Sunny-Side Up Sidecar (1 white)
Swedish Egg Coffee

2 EGGS

Aioli (2 yolks)
Asparagus and Parmesan Omelet
Asparagus with Hollandaise and a Fried Egg
Baked Macaroni and Cheese
Béarnaise Sauce (2 yolks)
Bread Pudding
Browned Butter Vanilla Cream Pudding (2 yolks)
Cardamom Streusel Blueberry Muffins
Classic French Trifold "Omelette"
Creamy Spiced Rice Pudding with Orange Sauce (2 yolks)
Crème Anglaise (2 yolks)
Eggs in a Nest
Fancy Rolled Sugar Cookies

Fig French Toast Sandwich
Fluffy Vanilla Pancakes
Fried Egg on Buttered Avocado Toast
Homemade Marshmallows (2 whites)
Lemon Blueberry Whoopie Pies
Maple Walnut Cake with Cream Cheese Frosting
Pancakes with Strawberries, Basil, and Cream
Peanut Butter and Jelly Sandwich Cookies
Peanut Butter Cookies
Rustic Open-Faced Egg Sandwich
Spinach and Goat Cheese Omelet
Tiramisu (2 yolks)
Vanilla Pudding (2 yolks)

3 EGGS

Blueberry Eton Mess (3 whites)
Butter Crackers
Caesar Dressing (3 yolks)
Cheesecake with Shortbread Crust
Cheesy Mushroom Pie (2 eggs and 1 yolk)
Chocolate Pots de Crème (3 yolks)
Finnish Egg Butter Spread
Hollandaise Sauce (3 yolks)
Lemon Caper Garlic Mayonnaise (3 yolks)
Lemon Curd
Marshmallow Crème (3 whites)

Homemade Mayonnaise (3 yolks)
Mini-Meringues (3 whites)
Mixed Berry Meringue Nests (3 whites)
Orange Brandy Olive Oil Cake
Pulla Bread
Pumpkin Swirl Cheesecake with Candied Walnuts
Ricotta Gnocchi (3 yolks)
Roasted Rhubarb Clafoutis
Royal Icing (3 whites)
Spicy Sriracha Mayonnaise (3 yolks)
Tartar Sauce (3 yolks)

4 EGGS

Baked Eggs Marinara
Blueberry Popovers
Cardamom Half-Pound Loaf Cake
Chimichurri Scrambled Eggs
Cloud Eggs
Cream-Fried Eggs
Cream Puffs
Crispy Lemon-Fried Eggs
Double Dill Scrambled Eggs
Eggs in Pots
Fried Eggs with Apricot Jam and Goat Cheese
Grilled Cheese and Egg Sandwich
Holiday Cranberry Half-Pound Cake
Homemade Pasta (3 eggs and 1 yolk)
Lemon Meringue Pie
Lemony Egg Salad Sandwich with Pesto and
   Avocado
Maple Chai Cream Puffs
Mint White Chocolate Ice Cream (4 yolks)
Niçoise Salad
Pasta Carbonara (4 yolks)
Ricotta Scrambled Eggs
Sabayon (4 yolks)
Scrambled-Egg Hand Pies
Skillet-Baked Bacon and Eggs
Toad-in-the-Hole
Vanilla Ice Cream (4 yolks)
Warm Bacon and Eggs Salad

5 EGGS

Bacon and Eggs Pizza
Broccoli Cheddar Tart
Gruyère Gougères (4 eggs and 1 yolk)
Rum Plum Breton (1 egg and 4 yolks)

6 EGGS

Baked Eggs in Butternut Squash Rings
Boozy Spiced Eggnog
Classic Quiche (5 eggs and 1 yolk)
Egg Lemon Soup (Avgolemono)
Lemon-Basil Bars
Pannukakku (Finnish Oven Pancake)
Savory Cheese Soufflés
Swiss Meringue Buttercream Frosting (6 whites)
Tomato Caprese Quiche (5 eggs and 1 yolk)
Vanilla Pastry Cream (6 yolks)

7 EGGS

Chocolate Cupcakes with Chocolate Swiss
   Meringue Buttercream Frosting (1 egg, 1 yolk,
   and 6 whites)
Easter Egg Braid
Eggs Benedict (4 eggs and 3 yolks)

8 EGGS

Bacon and Beet Hash
Bundt Pound Cake
Cheesy Baked Cream Eggs
Crème Brûlée (8 yolks)
Deviled Eggs with Avocado Oil and Sage
Deviled Eggs with Turmeric
Egg Drop Soup
Goat Cheese Frittata with Herbs
Maple Bacon Scotch Eggs
Toasty Holiday Strata

9 EGGS

Boston Cream Pie (3 eggs and 6 yolks)
No-Roll Vanilla Cookies, with frosting (2 eggs and
   7 whites)
Puffy Eggs

12 EGGS

Angel Food Cake (12 whites)
Sweet-Potato Sausage Frittata
Toasty Baked Egg Cups

13 EGGS

Egg Yolk Ravioli (12 eggs and 1 white)

INDEX

ABOUT THE AUTHOR

Lisa Steele is an author, popular television and radio guest, and creator of the blog *Fresh Eggs Daily*, the premiere online resource for chicken-keeping advice. Lisa has amassed an audience of nearly one million from all over the globe, who look to her for tips on raising backyard poultry naturally, gardening tips, and her coop-to-kitchen recipes. Her previous books on chicken keeping have sold more than 125,000 copies worldwide and are among the bestselling chicken-keeping books in print.

Dubbed "queen of the coop" by the media, Lisa has been recognized by many national media outlets, including the *Wall Street Journal*, *Forbes*, *USA Today*, *Country Living*, *Farmers' Almanac*, and *Parade*. As a television and radio personality, Lisa has appeared on the Hallmark Channel's *Home & Family*, *Martha Knows Best* on HGTV, *P. Allen Smith's Garden Home*, and NPR's *Maine Calling*. Her first book was recommended summer reading on *The View* in 2018, and her website was featured on an episode of *The Dr. Oz Show* that was focused on eating eggs. Lisa also hosted two seasons of the Telly Award–winning television show, *Welcome to My Farm*, on NBC in Maine.

A fifth-generation chicken keeper and Maine Master Gardener, Lisa lives in rural Maine, with her husband, their corgi and barn cat, and her "girls"—a mixed flock of about thirty hens, ducks, and geese. Plus one fairly grumpy rooster and a drake named Gregory.